ClearRevise™

BTEC Level 1/2 Tech Award
Digital Information Technology

Component 3:
Effective Digital Working Practices

Illustrated revision and practice

Published by
PG Online Limited
The Old Coach House
35 Main Road
Tolpuddle
Dorset
DT2 7EW
United Kingdom

sales@pgonline.co.uk
www.pgonline.co.uk
www.clearrevise.com
2020

PG ONLINE

PREFACE

Absolute clarity! That's the aim.

This is everything you need to ace your exam and beam with pride. Each topic is laid out in a beautifully illustrated format that is clear, approachable and as concise and simple as possible.

Each section of the specification is clearly indicated to help you cross-reference your revision. The checklist on the contents pages will help you keep track of what you have already worked through and what's left before the big day.

We have included worked examination-style questions and case studies with answers for almost every topic. This helps you understand where marks are coming from and to see the theory at work for yourself in an examination situation. There is also a set of exam-style questions at the end of each section for you to practise writing answers for. You can check your answers against those given at the end of the book.

LEVELS OF LEARNING

Based on the degree to which you are able to truly understand a new topic, we recommend that you work in stages. Start by reading a short explanation of something, then try and recall what you've just read. This has limited effect if you stop there but it aids the next stage. Question everything. Write down your own summary and then complete and mark a related exam-style question. Cover up the answers if necessary, but learn from them once you've seen them. Lastly, teach someone else. Explain the topic in a way that they can understand. Have a go at the different practice questions and case studies – they offer an insight into how and where marks are awarded.

ACKNOWLEDGEMENTS

The questions in the ClearRevise textbook are the sole responsibility of the authors and have neither been provided nor approved by the examination board.

Every effort has been made to trace and acknowledge ownership of copyright. The publishers will be happy to make any future amendments with copyright owners that it has not been possible to contact. The publisher would like to thank the following companies and individuals who granted permission for the use of their images in this textbook.

Design and artwork: Jessica Webb / PG Online Ltd
Graphics / images: © Shutterstock

First edition 2020. 10 9 8 7 6 5 4 3 2 1
A catalogue entry for this book is available from the British Library
ISBN: 978-1-910523-26-1
Copyright © PG Online 2020
All rights reserved

THE SCIENCE OF REVISION

Illustrations and words

Research has shown that revising with words and pictures doubles the quality of responses by students.[1] This is known as 'dual-coding' because it provides two ways of fetching the information from our brain. The improvement in responses is particularly apparent in students when asked to apply their knowledge to different problems. Recall, application and judgement are all specifically and carefully assessed in public examination questions.

Retrieval of information

Retrieval practice encourages students to come up with answers to questions.[2] The closer the question is to one you might see in a real examination, the better. Also, the closer the environment in which a student revises is to the 'examination environment', the better. Students who had a test 2–7 days away did 30% better using retrieval practice than students who simply read, or repeatedly reread material. Students who were expected to teach the content to someone else after their revision period did better still.[3] What was found to be most interesting in other studies is that students using retrieval methods and testing for revision were also more resilient to the introduction of stress.[4]

Ebbinghaus' forgetting curve and spaced learning

Ebbinghaus' 140-year-old study examined the rate in which we forget things over time. The findings still hold true. However, the act of forgetting things and relearning them is what cements things into the brain.[5] Spacing out revision is more effective than cramming – we know that, but students should also know that the space between revisiting material should vary depending on how far away the examination is. A cyclical approach is required. An examination 12 months away necessitates revisiting covered material about once a month. A test in 30 days should have topics revisited every 3 days – intervals of roughly a tenth of the time available.[6]

Summary

Students: the more tests and past questions you do, in an environment as close to examination conditions as possible, the better you are likely to perform on the day. If you prefer to listen to music while you revise, tunes without lyrics will be far less detrimental to your memory and retention. Silence is most effective.[5] If you choose to study with friends, choose carefully – effort is contagious.[7]

1.   Mayer, R. E., & Anderson, R. B. (1991). Animations need narrations: An experimental test of dual-coding hypothesis. *Journal of Education Psychology*, (83)4, 484–490.

2.   Roediger III, H. L., & Karpicke, J.D. (2006). Test-enhanced learning: Taking memory tests improves long-term retention. *Psychological Science*, 17(3), 249–255.

3.   Nestojko, J., Bui, D., Kornell, N. & Bjork, E. (2014). Expecting to teach enhances learning and organisation of knowledge in free recall of text passages. *Memory and Cognition*, 42(7), 1038–1048.

4.   Smith, A. M., Floerke, V. A., & Thomas, A. K. (2016) Retrieval practice protects memory against acute stress. *Science*, 354(6315), 1046–1048.

5.   Perham, N., & Currie, H. (2014). Does listening to preferred music improve comprehension performance? *Applied Cognitive Psychology*, 28(2), 279–284.

6.   Cepeda, N. J., Vul, E., Rohrer, D., Wixted, J. T. & Pashler, H. (2008). Spacing effects in learning a temporal ridgeline of optimal retention. *Psychological Science*, 19(11), 1095–1102.

7.   Busch, B. & Watson, E. (2019), *The Science of Learning*, 1st ed. Routledge.

CONTENTS

Section A   Modern technologies

Section B   Cyber security

Section C   The wider implications of digital systems

☑

Section D   Planning and communication in digital systems

☑

COMMAND VERBS

The exam paper that you take will use the following command verbs in each question. You may understand lots about a topic, but if you do not answer each question in the correct way, the mark you get may be lower than expected. Study each of the command verbs below along with their meanings and understand how they are used to answer a question.

Give / State / Name

Recall something that you know. These are short answers with 1 mark for each point.

Give three types of malware. [3]

Virus(1), Trojan(1), spyware(1).

Identify

Select some key information from something you are given.

Mia uses her home computer to go on the Internet.

Identify **one** item of network equipment that Mia uses. [1]

A router.(1)

Explain

An explain question needs two parts. First give an example and then give a reason why this example answers the question. Make sure to use words like 'because' or 'so' in this type of question.

Cecilia is concerned about her customers' personal data being stolen from her laptop.

Explain **one** security feature Cecilia should use to protect her data. [2]

She should encrypt the hard drive(1) so that if the computer is stolen, the thief won't be able to understand the data on it(1).

Example   Reason

Describe

Give an account of something.

This will often be the steps in a process.

Milo wishes to start his own online shop. He needs to collect personal customer data.

Describe the actions he must take before collecting personal data. [3]

Register with the Information Commissioner's Office.(1)

Make sure his customer database is secure.(1)

Create a privacy policy for the website.(1)

Annotate the diagram to explain how...

Label the diagram and add an explanation for each label.

Janice has a laptop, tablet and smartphone. Label the diagram to show how these can all connect to the same Internet connection.

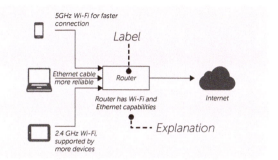

5GHz Wi-Fi for faster connection

Label

Ethernet cable more reliable

Router

Router has Wi-Fi and Ethernet capabilities

Internet

Explanation

2.4 GHz Wi-Fi, supported by more devices

Assess

1) Write down all the factors or events that apply.

2) Identify those that are most important.

3) Assess the importance of the factors.

4) Give a conclusion.

You should use full paragraphs in your answers.

A full answer will usually be around a page of text.

A company wants staff to use their smartphones to monitor their social media accounts.

Assess the impact of smartphone use for monitoring social media accounts.

You must provide a conclusion as to whether you think that providing smartphones for this use is a good idea. [8]

Monitoring social media accounts on a smartphone will encourage staff to work whilst at home as the devices will constantly be giving notifications for new posts. This is a serious problem as it will affect their work-life balance.

Relevant factor

Importance of the factor

Detailed knowledge

The company could mitigate the work-life balance problem by explaining to staff when they should and shouldn't be monitoring the accounts.

Clear link to previous point

In conclusion, this is only a good idea if the company makes it clear when they should be used. Even then, they should make sure that staff agree to the request before implementing it.

Conclusion is based on the assessment

Discuss

Identify the problem or issue in the question.

Explore the relevant points that relate to the problem or issue with logical thoughts or arguments.

You should use full paragraphs to answer these questions.

The full answer will usually be around a page of text.

Virtual PA provide laptops and headsets to all their remote workers.

Discuss how remote workers can help protect the environment. [6]

They could change the power settings so that the displays turn to suspend mode if the computer hasn't been used for 10 minutes. The hard disk platters could also be made to stop spinning.

Accurate knowledge

Detailed knowledge

As remote workers pay for their own electricity they would have the incentive of lower energy bills and the result would be a reduced impact on the environment.

Relevant to the question context

Clear links between points

Draw

Draw a process using a data flow diagram, information flow diagram or flowchart.

The drawing should be labelled and annotated.

A health app has the number of steps a user walks as an input. It then calculates the number of miles walked and outputs it.

Draw a flowchart of this process.

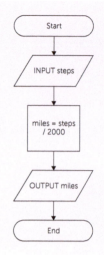

Evaluate

Give a logical evaluation that considers different and competing points. Include strengths, weaknesses, relevant data or information.

Give a conclusion that is supported by the evaluation.

You should use full paragraphs to answer these questions.

The full answer will usually be around a page of text.

SmartGym want all their personal trainers to have a computer device. The options are a smartphone, tablet or laptop.

Evaluate the advantages and disadvantages of the different devices, stating which would be best for their personal trainers to use.

A Smartphone is small and portable meaning that it can be used when monitoring people as they train. It makes use of modern wireless Wi-Fi standards which enables it to be connected to a network via a wireless access point. Smartphones have small screens, which makes it hard to show results or video to their clients. ...

•----- Advantages

•----- Relevant to the question context

•----- Detailed knowledge

•----- Detailed understanding

•----- Disadvantages

In conclusion, a tablet would be the best device as it offers portability and a screen size that can display more content.

•----- Conclusion

MARK ALLOCATIONS

Green mark allocations[1] on answers to in-text questions throughout this guide help to indicate where marks are gained within the answers. A bracketed '1' e.g. [1] = one valid point worthy of a mark. In longer answer questions, a mark is given based on the whole response. In these answers, a tick mark[✓] indicates that a valid point has been made. There are often many more points to make than there are marks available so you have more opportunity to max out your answers than you may think.

TOPICS FOR COMPONENT 3
EFFECTIVE DIGITAL WORKING PRACTICES

Information about the externally assessed exam

Written exam: 1 hour 30 minutes
60 marks
All questions are mandatory
40% of qualification grade

Specification coverage

Modern technologies, cyber security, the wider implications of digital systems and planning and communication in digital systems.

The content for this assessment will be drawn from the essential subject content sections A to D of Component 3 in the specification.

Questions

A mix of short answer and longer answer questions assessing knowledge, understanding and skills in contextual scenarios building on all components within the qualification.

SETTING UP AD HOC NETWORKS

An ad hoc network is a temporary network that connects two or more computers or devices. An ad hoc network is commonly used to connect a device whilst on the move. This could be done via an open Wi-Fi network or a personal hotspot.

An ad hoc network requires no additional specialist hardware (such as a router) making them easy to connect to and set up However, as these types of networks get bigger, they may be difficult to manage without any central control.

Open Wi-Fi

An open **Wi-Fi** network may be provided by a company, a town council or a school for example. It is commonly a free service that creates a Wi-Fi network that anyone can connect to as and when they come and go.

Tethering / Personal hotspot

A **personal hotspot** is an **ad hoc Wi-Fi network** created using a mobile device such as a smart phone. The device will connect to the data network using the cellular phone network's 4G or 5G connection. A very local Wi-Fi network is then created using a Bluetooth connection from the phone to which you may connect or **tether** another device such as a laptop. This is useful when there are no other reliable Wi-Fi connections available.

A **personal area network** (**PAN**) can be created by pairing devices together via **Bluetooth** or **Wi-Fi**. Generally, these pairings work within a very small range of up to 10 metres. They are commonly used with hands free phone systems or smart speakers.

1. Amy is looking to connect to an open Wi-Fi network. Give **two** common places Amy should look for an open network. [2]

   Hotels[1], transport hubs such as stations or airports[1], trains[1], coach services[1] and cafés[1].

2. Jamil is a journalist reporting from a remote location with no Internet connection. He is required to send his report to Head Office from his laptop. He has a smartphone with a good signal.

   Explain how Jamil could send the report electronically. [2]

   He can tether his laptop to his phone / create a mobile hotspot[1]. His laptop can then use his phone's Internet connection[1].

NETWORK SECURITY AND PERFORMANCE

Security issues with open networks

Open networks are typically less secure than private networks. All data on an **unsecured** network is sent unencrypted. This means that anyone who intercepts data that is sent across the network can read and understand it. This includes passwords and credit card numbers for example.

WPA encryption (**Wi-Fi Protected Access**) should be used with Wi-Fi networks to prevent any data from being understood if it is intercepted.

Performance issues with ad hoc networks

Network performance can suffer as a result of the volume of data being transferred across it. If there are many users on the same network, each downloading video, performance is going to be very slow. Mobile hotspots support up to 11 Mbps (megabits per second) whereas standard Wi-Fi supports 54 Mbps or higher. **Mobile speeds** are increasing constantly and 5G aims to offer a much faster data transfer rate which can also cope with many more users.

3. Terry is using an unencrypted open network to access an email in his email account.

Explain **one** reason why he shouldn't access his account without suitable security. [2]

The username and password to access his email account will be sent over an unencrypted network[1] which will allow an eavesdropper/hacker to read them both[1].

If the username and password are obtained due to it being an unencrypted network[1] then a hacker will easily be able to look at Terry's emails to find personal information and passwords[1] that can be used to steal money / commit fraud[1].

ISSUES AFFECTING NETWORK AVAILABILITY

The availability of networking connections can be affected by various factors.

Developed vs developing countries

Developing countries have far less networking **infrastructure** than **developed countries** but mobile and satellite technology is helping where cable networks cannot reach. This, however, can be expensive to use and many areas are still without mains electricity to power connections.

Network availability

In the UK, some rural areas have limited access to fibre **broadband**. Towns and cities have generally faster connections and can increasingly access **fibre** directly to the home. In the UK, most 'fibre' connections make use of **fibre to the cabinet** (**FTTC**) which has a **copper** connection from the home to the **cabinet** and then a fibre connection from the cabinet to the **exchange**.

Mobile coverage

The **cellular network** divides the UK into cells with a mobile **base station** transmitter in each cell. A cell without a **transmitter** is likely to have no signal or a poor one from a neighbouring cell.

Rural vs city locations

Cities and **urban areas** tend to have many more **open networks** available to use than rural areas. They can expect greater numbers of people to use the service so it is worth the set up and maintenance costs of providing it. This infrastructure is not always worth the investment in rural areas. Many **rural areas** rely on the mobile phone network for their data connection. Commonly, they will use a **4G** or **5G dongle**.

Mobile blackspots

Hills and large buildings can cast 'shadows' by absorbing radio signals, causing apparent mobile **blackspots**.

CASE STUDY

Lucy lives in a rural location and works for a fashion retailer. She often needs to fly abroad to India.

She will need to use her laptop and smartphone in both rural factories and hotels as well as the company head office in London.

Discuss the issues Lucy may have with ad hoc networks and open networks. [6]

- Lucy's home network in the countryside may have limited **infrastructure**, so she may find **video conferencing** difficult if she has only a slow **copper connection**. She may need to use **mobile broadband** using a **4G connection**, but there may be issues here with **mobile blackspots**. Before purchasing, she will need to check the network coverage to see if she will have a signal.

- If she gets the train to the airport or head office, she could use her mobile broadband to continue doing her work. She will also need to be able to work offline in case she goes into a **blackspot** or through a tunnel.

- At head office, the infrastructure may include a very fast **fibre optic connection**. This would be the best place to upload and download videos or large files if possible, and to resynchronise any files she has worked on offline from the cloud.

- If she wants to work when flying, she won't have an Internet connection. She will need to download any files she needs from the **cloud** to her local computer in advance.

- Many of the locations of factories in India are likely to be **rural**. Whilst they may have good Internet connections, unless she knows otherwise, she should anticipate no, or very slow, Internet. As such, she should be able to store any **work offline** until she returns to a hotel room with a signal.

- She should take an ethernet cable to connect to the hotel as well as having a Wi-Fi enabled laptop and phone. This will give her the maximum chance of connecting to the hotel's Internet.

- When connecting to the hotel Wi-Fi, she needs to consider that the network may be open and is therefore a security risk.

- She should use a **Virtual Private Network (VPN)** connection to encrypt all communications with the Internet.

- If she can get **mobile Internet** on her phone using a **4G data connection** then she will be able to **tether** her laptop to it using **Bluetooth**.

- Before she books any hotel, she may want to check they have an Internet connection and that it has **sufficient bandwidth** for the Internet use that she will require. This will be very important if she wants to send back videos of products or issues in the factories.

Long answers must be written in paragraphs. Bullet points have been used here to make the answers easier to understand. This type of question will be marked using a Levels Based Marks Scheme. See page 76 for details.

CLOUD STORAGE AND COMPUTING

The **Cloud** is a term used for a service accessible via the **Internet**. Services that are offered via the cloud include cloud storage and cloud computing.

Cloud storage allows users to store files on remote **servers**. **Cloud computing** enables software applications to reside in the cloud where processing can be carried out on more powerful computers than a local machine.

Name	Access rights		
Karson Webber	View	Edit	Owner
Alisha Cotton	View	Edit	
Matthew Dupont	View		
Gladys Deacon	View		

Features and usage of cloud storage

- **Access rights** can be set up to allow different people different levels of use. Basic access rights can be configured as Read only, Read and Write (or Edit) and Full access which enables such a user to edit the access rights of others.

- Data is **available 24/7** from any computer in the world with a good Internet connection.

- **Backups** are automatically done by the provider which means that users don't need to buy additional storage devices to backup data nor do users need to remember to back it up.

- Cloud storage is more **scalable**. Flexible **storage capacity** means users only pay for the data that they use allowing them to increase their storage only as they need it. This saves money on buying separate hardware. The provider may charge a higher fee to store more data, but these costs will come down again as data is deleted.

- All files are stored online and **synchronised** with connected devices. Offline files can be updated which then automatically resynchronise as soon as a connection is restored.

- The provider will configure the system and all of the storage devices, so users do not need their own **maintenance** team.

- **Support** is often available to resolve **technical issues** quickly.

Cloud storage providers include Dropbox, OneDrive and Google Drive.

Data centres

A **data centre** is a large temperature-controlled building that houses computer servers. Professional engineers will maintain the hardware. Data centres will have multiple Internet connections and backup electricity supplies from generators or **UPS** (**Uninterruptible Power Supply**) batteries. This allows them to have almost no **downtime** meaning you have access to files or online services whenever you need them.

1. Give **two** security methods a data centre will use to protect your data. [2]

   Door entry locks[1], biometrics[1], security staff[1], CCTV[1], Fire protection systems[1], secondary backup generators[1], offsite backups[1].

Cloud computing

Online applications are stored in, and accessed, via the cloud. This saves space on a local machine or smartphone and takes advantage of greater **processing power** on **cloud servers**. Common examples of cloud-based software include **accounting packages**, **customer relationship management systems** and general purpose application software such as **Office 365** or **Google Docs**. Online software provides **automatic updates** to all users which reduces issues of incompatibility and makes sure everyone is using the latest version and features.

2. Mina runs a small training organisation with four trainers each covering different parts of the UK. She is considering employing further trainers on a remote working basis. Discuss how online applications could benefit Mina and her team. [6]

Software will be continuously updated so that everyone is using the latest versions[✓]. This helps with the compatibility and consistency of versions between users.[✓] Files can be shared with other members of the team via a cloud-based platform.[✓] Many platforms also allow collaborative working so that more than one user can view and edit the same file at the same time.[✓] Messaging and chat features can help maintain communication between the team.[✓] Video conferencing facilities can allow for face-to-face meetings and screen sharing.[✓] Trainers can access their files, software and chat applications from any computer in the world with an Internet connection.[✓] This enables them more flexibility in where they can work[✓] and Mina may be able to expand the team and the training coverage they can provide more easily[✓]. New users can be added very easily.[✓]

Refer to the levels based mark scheme on page 76.

Collaboration tools

1. **Live** or **real-time** chat-based workspaces such as Microsoft Teams and Zoom enable **instant messaging**, **screen sharing** and **video conferencing** facilities.

2. Groups can be set up so that files and projects can be shared between particular members of a larger team.

3. **Real-time co-authoring** enables more than one user to work on and edit the same document at the same time, from different devices. All users can see who is writing what, live on screen.

4. **Comments** can be added to documents. **Track changes** will allow a history of changes and which users made them to be seen.

SELECTION OF PLATFORMS AND SERVICES

A **computer platform** comprises the **hardware**, **software** and **operating system** that runs on it. Examples of popular platforms include a PC running Windows 10, a smartphone running Android or an Apple computer running macOS.

Cloud platforms, such as Amazon Web Services (AWS), provide a platform for **developers** to put their **cloud applications** on. These platforms give access to almost unlimited storage and **processing** capabilities. As such they are known as **scalable**. A small start-up company could rent access to a cloud platform's services which would decrease their initial hardware and maintenance costs. If their business is very successful it will be very easy to scale by renting more **virtual storage** or processing power.

Some **software as a service** (**SaaS**) may be more suitable for a mobile platform, others for desktop computers, whilst many are cross-platform so that they can be viewed on any device.

Number and complexity of features

Online services tend to offer features that are not always available with offline counterparts.

Features include:

- **Collaborative working** and a more seamless experience as users move between devices.
- **Autosaving files** and settings with a version history available to look back through.
- **Different users may have different access rights** to features. For example, **age filtering** is used on streamed content by user account for family services such as Netflix and YouTube. In a company, a receptionist may be prevented from accessing the accounts software.

When choosing a cloud platform or service, consideration needs to be made for:

- The amount of storage given to each user and whether there will be a large increase in fees if more is needed later.
- The security of the data stored by the provider and whether this is sufficient to protect personal information under the Data Protection Act.
- The frequency of updates for security patches or new features and the amount of downtime that will result when these are carried out.

Interface design

Interface design on different devices is crucial to the overall user experience, especially if users are likely to use more than one to access the service. This includes the **layout** of the screen information and a consideration of input. For example, an app to select photos on a PC may allow many photos to be selected with a mouse. Whilst the equivalent app on a smartphone may display only a few photos due to the smaller display size. These will be selected using the touchscreen. Other features that may be available on some platforms include microphones for voice control or GPS for location data. People who have accessibility issues such as sight or hearing loss, or a physical impairment will also need to be able to use a platform to access the same services.

Paid for versus free services

Free versions of cloud services often provide a way to attract new customers with a limited service. This may be time limited, feature limited, space limited or device limited. Once a premium fee is paid, users may be able to access more features on more devices, or they may see an advert-free version. Business versions also have a **commercial licence** for a higher fee.

Paid for applications are not always better. Careful consideration needs to be made. For instance, G Suite for Education is free for schools and may have better **ease of use** and collaborative features than many paid for cloud or offline **productivity tools** available. Linux is an operating system that is free but very reliable and allows developers to customise how it works. However, as it is free, support needs to be purchased which may make it more costly for some businesses than operating systems such as Windows.

Available devices

Software will often be built to run on different hardware platforms. Many will offer seamless use from one device to another as a user pauses a program or saves work on one device to resume playback or editing at exactly the same point on another device later.

However, some software will not be suited to some devices. For example, Serif Affinity Photo is photo editing software. It is available for the macOS and Windows desktop platforms. It is also available for the iPadOS platform for Apple tablets. However, it isn't available for the iOS smartphone or Android platforms as they have smaller screen sizes.

Noah is looking for an online music-streaming service to use with his home stereo speaker, smartphone and wireless headphones.

Explain **two** features of the service that Noah should look out for when selecting a provider. [4]

The ability to save music offline[1] will enable Noah to listen to music on his phone in places that do not have a reliable signal[1]. Services that allow Noah to seamlessly transfer music playback from one device to another[1] would enable him to continue to listen to a song when he leaves the house by transferring it to his mobile phone[1]. The service needs to be able to stream at varying bitrates[1] so that Noah can listen in high quality at home / a lower bit-rate on his mobile to reduce his data charges[1]. Noah should consider whether he wants a subscription service[1] or to be able to buy songs that will then have no further costs[1].

USING SYSTEMS TOGETHER

Device synchronisation

With **device synchronisation**, any files, photos, documents or settings created or edited on one device will automatically update to one central cloud location. Once updated, all other connected devices will see the latest additions or changes. For instance, when a photo is taken on an Apple iPhone it can automatically be sent to Apple's iCloud. It is then sent to other devices linked to the account such as an iPad tablet or iMac desktop. If one of these devices deletes the photo then it will be deleted from all other devices.

Notifications

Notifications can be set up to inform you of recent changes to files by other members of the same team, conflicted copies or synchronisation issues. For instance, if two different users both edit the same file, a notification may ask which file should be kept when they are uploaded.

Online/offline working

Many people find that they need to use laptops or mobile devices in places where an Internet connection is not available. This is known as offline working. For instance, a surveyor may be looking at building plans at a building site that has no communications infrastructure or they may be taking measurements in the countryside.

Services such as Dropbox save a copy of all their files on a local laptop or tablet. If any changes are made to a file, the new version will be uploaded and synchronised to the cloud as soon as an Internet connection is available. The latest version of the file can also be shared with others in the organisation.

Mary is planning to work on company files saved on a cloud service provider whilst travelling to a meeting via train.

Explain why Mary will need a cloud service that still works when she is offline.   [2]

Access to online files on the train may be limited by poor Internet connection, if any.[1] So if the cloud service doesn't store a copy of the files she is working on locally, she will not be able to access or complete her work.[1] If a cloud service operates solely online, then she may lose any work she has not saved if a connection is lost[1] or she may not be able to complete any further work until the connection is restored.[1]

IMPLICATIONS FOR ORGANISATIONS WHEN CHOOSING CLOUD TECHNOLOGIES

Choosing the right **cloud technology** can make the difference between success or failure for an organisation. Implementation can be expensive and cause interruption so getting things right first time is important.

Disaster recovery

The loss of IT services or company files can be catastrophic for an organisation. Some companies may never recover again unless all eventualities have been planned for. Disaster may come in the form of:

- Loss of data from theft, corruption, a malware attack, accidental deletion or simply a loss of access.
- Natural disaster, for example, fire or flood.
- Loss of staff with technical expertise.

Cloud technology providers have procedures to protect the data that they store, but their users still need to reassure themselves that they are well protected by these policies. Cloud providers will hold copies of the data on more than one hard drive in different locations. This is known as **redundancy**. This means that if one hard drive fails or is destroyed in one location, another can immediately be used.

Procedures for accessing data and backups should be carefully analysed before choosing a cloud provider. Whilst a backup of data may be available from a cloud provider, if it can only be downloaded at 5 Mbps and there is 1 TB (Terabyte) of data in the backup, then it will take over 18 days to restore the data. This could easily be long enough for a business to go bankrupt. However, it if only a few files need to be retrieved, this may be possible in minutes.

Security of data

Data is crucial to most organisations' survival. It may be sensitive or even sentimental for individuals too. For this reason, backup copies of data should be stored at multiple different locations and encrypted. Data centres will typically have **CCTV**, **security guards** and **fire suppression systems**. The policies and procedures of any cloud storage provider should be checked carefully to ensure they have sufficient security in place and to assess useful additional features such as **historical version recovery**. The ability to select which countries the data can be stored in will also help ensure compliance with the Data Protection Act.

Explain why backup data should be stored away from the original versions of the files.   [2]

Should any natural disaster, theft or electromagnetic pulse affect the data held on one site[1], it is unlikely that an alternative site would suffer the same event[1].

CLOUD SERVICE CONSIDERATIONS

Compatibility

Cloud platforms will typically allow Microsoft Windows or Linux to be installed. These are both commonly used operating systems in industry which leads to fewer compatibility issues. However, any software as a service will need to make sure that it is compatible with all of the different platforms that users may use, for example, PC, Mac and Android.

A web development company could run the WordPress web content management software on any cloud provider that offers Windows or Linux on their servers.

Maintenance

Cloud storage and computing facilities are maintained by highly experienced engineers. They aim to make services or data available with **uptimes** commonly above 99.9%. That equates to roughly one minute of downtime per day, or 1 hour of **downtime** per month.

System administrators will have access to information such as **server outages**, alerts or **network connection** issues.

Getting a service or storage facility up and running quickly

If a new business wanted to set up a new productivity suite and backup system in house, they would need to purchase servers and computers, install the operating systems and software, and then configure and test the system. Security precautions such as firewalls would also need to be put in place. This technology would typically need a specialist technician to be employed. For even a small business this could take weeks. By contrast, setting up a cloud service system such as G Suite or Office 365 could be achieved in minutes by simply selecting which services are required for the company and making a card payment.

Performance considerations

Cloud-based software needs to perform as well as any locally installed software to prevent any time delay in processing requests. Companies and their customers need to feel that the systems they use are **responsive**.

A fast and reliable **broadband** connection is the most crucial component to the success of cloud software or storage. Upload and download speeds need to be fast to make collaborative working smoother. Some businesses will have more than one Internet connection so that if one fails, their systems can make use of the other.

A cloud service may be shared with many different customers. This could result in the service slowing down when many people use it. Equally, some online services may initially be cheap, but as the business expands, they become progressively more expensive. Once a business is using a system it can be hard to change, so this should be carefully considered before any decision to buy.

DAILY NEWS

Word · Business · Finance · Lifestyle · Travel · Sport · Weather

№ 7674177203

THOUSANDS LOST IN DOWNTIME

DECEMBER 2019

Downtime of unplanned maintenance o_ website server costs local Cardiff busine__ hour. The online sales company was for__ trading for the duration of the downtime_ loss of revenue.

WORLD NEWS

100 million credit card details stolen

JULY 2019

Capital One Financial has had a massive data breach of 100 million credit card details. The data was stored with Amazon Web Services (AWS). The hacker got in through a web app running on AWS that had a firewall misconfiguration. Almost $2 billion was wiped off Capital One's share price as a result.

NEWS

FIRE DESTROYS SCHOOL

AUGUST 2016

A West Sussex secondary school fire has damaged buildings containing the school's servers. The school had made use of cloud storage to backup over 1TB of student and staff data including GCSE coursework. All data was restored from the cloud within 10 hours.

AdSoft recently lost all of its sales data owing to accidental deletion.

Explain **one** way in which the risk of accidental deletion of data can be reduced. [2]

An onscreen alert could be used[1] to ask for confirmation that the files should be deleted.[1] Staff should be trained[1] to know that the deletion of the wrong files could have serious implications for the company.[1] Access levels[1] could prevent staff having access to the files in the first place, or limit the access to read only.[1] Backups of the data[1] can allow for it to be restored if accidental deletion has occurred.[1]

CASE STUDY

Kevan manages a computer network for ABM, a small advertising company.

He is responsible for the safety and security of the network and the data held on its servers.

Discuss what considerations that Kevan may need to take in moving the company's email, backups and office suite to a cloud-based service. [6]

- ABM will need to have a **fast connection** so that there aren't any delays when editing documents and so that **collaborative features** work smoothly.

- Kevan may wish to consider whether ABM purchase a second Internet connection so that all systems will still work if one Internet connection is not working.

- Cloud service **backup procedures** will need to be checked. ABM will need to consider how often these are carried out, the locations of the backups and how long **restoring the data** will take.

- The **cloud service** needs to provide all of the **features** currently offered by their current systems and software, plus any others that may be required as they grow the company.

- The cloud software needs to be simple to use and run on **any platform** that staff or customers are likely to use. It may also need to be **responsive to different devices** and screen sizes.

- **Staff** will need to be **trained** to use the cloud-based software features including **collaborative working**, notification, messaging and **synchronisation** of files.

- **Outsourcing** all of the data on the servers to the cloud will reduce the number of staff required to manage the local servers, reducing company costs. However, these savings need to be compared against the ongoing costs of the cloud service and how this will increase as the company grows.

- As the technical administration will move to the cloud service provider, ABM will be protected against a loss of knowledge of the existing network set up if Kevan or other **key staff decide to leave**.

- An advertising company may be creating **large videos or graphics files**. The use of cloud software may make their processes much slower if they have a **slow connection**.

- The company needs to consider which country the data will be stored in and whether the protections of the cloud-provider will be strong enough to be **compliant** with the **Data Protection Act**.

- ABM will have less control over their email and need to check what happens if they are blocked by the cloud provider for spam.

- Cloud storage **software** will be **automatically upgraded** so there is no need to worry about installing newer versions manually.

Long answers must be written in paragraphs. Bullet points have been used here to make the answers easier to understand. This type of question will be marked using a Levels Based Marks Scheme. See page 76 for details.

EXAMINATION PRACTICE

Kate's Karting is a small karting circuit near Birmingham. Kate is the owner of the business. All company documents, photos and videos are stored offline on Kate's desktop computer.

(a) State **two** advantages of Kate moving to cloud storage. [2]

(b) State **two** disadvantages of Kate moving to cloud storage. [2]

(c) Currently, Kate deletes photos of races that are more than 30 days old as she has run out of storage space on her hard drive.

Explain how cloud storage may make it easier for Kate to keep photos. [2]

(d) Kate is concerned about her data being lost due to fire or flood if she stores it in the cloud. Explain why this is unlikely to be something that should concern her. [2]

Kate currently has a website that is used to give information to customers about the racing circuit and competitor achievements.

(e) Explain **two** ways in which the interface needs to be designed to take into account the variety of available devices that are likely to access the website. [4]

(f) The website asks users to enter information via a form. State **one** method of security that will help to keep the data entered safe from being intercepted. [1]

(g) Kate's website can get very busy on race days. Competitors and visitors will constantly refresh the results page, and this has led to the website running slow or crashing.

Describe how the use of cloud computing can help Kate's website cope better with this demand. [3]

Customers are currently making use of their own mobile data to access Kate's website when they are at the racetrack.

(h) A customer has a laptop that they wish to use to share race statistics that they have compiled.

Describe how it is possible for the customer to connect to the Internet using their laptop and smartphone. [2]

(i) Customers that use one particular mobile phone network have said that they have trouble using their phones to access the website.

Give **two** reasons why this may be the case. [2]

(j) Kate has decided that she would like to introduce an open Wi-Fi network for her racers and visitors to use. She is concerned about the security of their devices if they connect to it.

Explain **one** way that the network can be kept secure for her customers. [2]

CHANGES TO MODERN TEAMS

Modern technologies have changed the way in which teams from around the world can work together with complete flexibility.

Multi-cultural world teams

Bringing together people from all over the world into a single team enables a diverse range of ideas to flow. People from different **cultures** bring a **diverse** set of experiences which will benefit organisations, especially multinational companies. **Video conferencing** and instant messaging facilities bring everyone together without the need to travel.

Time zone differences between team members enable a team to work continuously on a project round-the-clock, passing projects from one team to the next throughout each day. There is no restriction on who can be involved in a team based on geographic location.

System administrator
Vancouver

London GMT
09:00–17:00 GMT

Shanghai GMT+8
17:00–01:00 GMT

Los Angeles GMT−8
01:00–09:00 GMT

Lead engineer
Mumbai

Front-end developer
Sydney

Permanent and casual staff

The flexibility given to companies by using modern technologies allows them to make greater use of **casual staff**, such as freelancers, rather than **permanent employees**. This benefits the company as they are able to easily increase the size of teams to complete projects. Whilst many freelancers may appreciate the flexibility, some people may dislike the insecurity of not having a permanent job.

Flexible working and inclusivity

Team members can work any time of day or night meaning that they can choose to work when they wish to with no set work hours. This is often referred to as **24/7/365**. It is also possible for them to be working in different **time zones**. This flexibility enables people to fit work more comfortably around their own lives. This often improves productivity and happiness.

Some team members may be permanent staff, other specialists may be brought in for part of a project where they are required. Some team members may be based in a central office; others may work from home. Remote working allows people who cannot work in an office to also be able to participate in teams. People with disabilities or those unable to travel can find **inclusion** in projects, enabling them to make a valuable contribution to the team and to society.

A company decides to enable all of its employees to work from home using modern technologies to communicate.

Explain **two** benefits to the company of allowing their employees to work remotely. [4]

Less office space is required[1] so the company saves on rent, heating and lighting costs.[1] Remote communications are more likely to be monitored[1] providing a record that can be viewed or listened to at a later date.[1] Employees are likely to be happier and have a better work-life balance[1] resulting in them being more productive so that the company is more profitable.[1] Employees no longer need to travel to work[1] resulting in their travel costs and time being saved[1]. There is access to a wider set of potential employees who could not ordinarily travel to the office[1] resulting in the ability of attracting employees with a more diverse skillset.[1]

MANAGING MODERN TEAMS

Modern technologies provide features to help manage a team that may be working remotely from each other.

Collaboration tools

Shared documents enable several people to work together on the same file at the same time, creating a single, consistent version. Any changes made by members of the collaborative team can be seen instantly as they are made. A record of who changed what is kept with the document and a **version history** is stored providing access to older versions of the file each time it was saved. Shared calendars allow events or entire calendars to be shared with others. This helps with scheduling tasks. Reminders can be set and the time shown will correspond with a person's local time zone.

Technologies such as blogs and wikis allow many users to edit web pages. Blogs (web logs) started as a way to record diary entries. However, the software to make them, such as WordPress has morphed into a way to collaboratively make websites. Around 35% of websites are produced using WordPress. Wikis allow users to very quickly add updates to a webpage. In Hawaiian, the word *wikiwiki* means speedy. Wikipedia is the most successful example of a website built on this technology. It is now the largest encyclopedia in the world, but users should be aware that anyone can edit it which may introduce errors or inaccuracies.

Communication tools

Communication tools include email, instant messaging, video conferencing, text messages and message boards. Instant messaging facilities such as Slack or Microsoft Teams provide an easy platform for questions and discussions to take place between colleagues, screen sharing and displaying user status.

Scheduling and planning tools

Scheduling and planning tools increase productivity and help organise tasks within the workplace. This may include to-do lists and calendars which notify users of an upcoming event, meeting or task that needs to be addressed.

Projects can be organised using many methods, two of which are Gantt charts or a Kanban system.

Kanban systems allow multiple users to create tasks and move them to different stages, known as buckets, according to progress. For example, a building company may have the following tasks: 'Sales call', 'Survey', 'Quote', 'Job in progress', 'Invoice'.

A Gantt chart shows subtasks of a project but takes into account the length of each job, project milestones, tasks that are dependent on the completion of others and the length of time allocated to each sub-task. Project management software using the Kanban system or Gantt charts can automatically notify group members of any tasks they have been assigned to.

COMMUNICATION WITH STAKEHOLDERS

A **stakeholder** is anyone who has an interest in an organisation or is affected by the decisions, actions or policies that it makes. Common stakeholders include **customers**, **suppliers** and **staff**. This may extend to shareholders, company owners and the government.

Communication platforms

Common **communication channels** include **websites**, **social media**, **email**, **live chat**, **video conferencing** and **telephone communication**. Companies may choose to use any or all of these methods to communicate with their stakeholders. A different selection may be used for each group of stakeholders, or for different types of communication – for example, customer queries may be handled through live chat on their website or social media such as Twitter or Facebook. A company may require an email or recorded phone call for complaints as these keep a clear record.

- **Social media** is a great tool for creating awareness of a company's goods or services. **Public status updates** allow the sharing of new offers or information about products and services. They allow a wide audience to see the messages. By contrast, a company may choose to use a **direct** or **private message** to resolve a private matter with a customer. Companies often promote themselves as knowledge leaders by posting the latest news on related topics. This increases **followers** and their **market awareness**. Social platforms are very widely adopted and can be used by customers to ask questions or communicate with a company. Organisations can then reply to customer questions, 'like' posts or retweet positive customer comments. Advertisers can target specific groups of people to maximise an advert's response.

- **Websites** are useful to allow people to browse a company's offering and read **reviews** from other users. For digital products, such as software, music and books, trial versions or samples can be given that enable customers to make informed choices without any pressure from a sales team. An **Intranet** could be used to communicate with staff.

- **Live chat** windows on websites provide customers with a way to obtain answers to any quick questions they may have. Generic responses from **chat bots** or computers can be infuriating for customers. The same is often true of automated phone systems.

- **Independent reviews** from social media platforms and from past customers via review sites are also useful in helping a customer to come to an informed decision.

- **Email** can be used to give further information or to send a quote to customer. A speedy and comprehensive response to an email enables a company to show the quality of their customer service.

- **Voice communication** can now be carried out by **telephone**, **mobile phone** or **VoIP (Voice over Internet Protocol)** phones. VoIP phones can be installed in seconds anywhere with an Internet connection giving employees the freedom to work anywhere in the world. Mobile phones allow people to have discussions away from offices and desks.

CASE STUDY

StarPlay Adventure is a company that makes wooden play equipment for gardens and playgrounds. They have a global team of designers, marketers, salespeople and factory workers.

They are having some difficulties with the planning of projects and communication between team members. At the moment they mainly use spreadsheets for project planning and telephones for communication. They are considering moving to online planning and communication tools.

Assess the use of online planning tools and more modern communication tools. **[9]**

- Online planning tools will allow all team **members** to be **assigned to tasks** that they are involved with.
- They will always be able to see the most up to date version of the project plan.
- If they are using **Gantt chart software**, this will always show when each part of the project ends.
- If one sub-task is delayed all other dependent tasks will instantly reflect this.
- People involved on projects or tasks can receive **automatic updates** on the project to their email. Managers can receive updates on project milestones.
- More modern communication tools include **video conferencing systems** that can help to show team members reactions to ideas.
- These systems run over the Internet so are far cheaper than telephone calls.
- They also allow many team members to be involved in each meeting.
- Company communication could be further improved by using **communication platforms** such as Teams or Slack.
- This type of software allows **chat rooms** or **threads** to be organised by topic or team.
- This allows discussions, questions and documents to be commented on by all members.
- Using such systems allows quick ideas and questions to be answered and discussed without the need for formal meetings to be scheduled – employee efficiency improves.
- **Direct messages** and video calls can instantly be had with required team members.
- There are disadvantages to the company using these systems. These include:
  - The need for **staff training** in the new systems which may be less productive initially.
  - Tools that are often highly dependent on a fast and **reliable Internet connection**. Some employees may live in an area with poor broadband. Other employees may be in a country that has less reliability or insufficient speed.
  - Requirements to plan more carefully for meetings as coworkers may be in different **time zones**.

Long answers must be written in paragraphs. Bullet points have been used here to make the answers easier to understand. This type of question will be marked using a Levels Based Marks Scheme. See page 76 for details.

INTERFACE DESIGN AND ACCESSIBILITY

Modern technologies can provide new ways to access data and information. It is important to consider the **accessibility** of technologies along with how they help organisations to be **inclusive**.

Communication platforms

The **layout**, **font** and **colour scheme** of a web page or software application can affect its usability. **Screen layout** should maximise the available visible area and use plenty of white space. **White space** is the part of the screen design that does not contain content. This may be in margins, between columns or around graphics. Screen content should also automatically adjust to fit the screen size and proportions of most common devices. This is known as **responsive design**.

Fonts

Fonts can affect readability. **Serif** fonts contain serifs which are small strokes at the ends of letters. This style of font tends to be harder to read on screen, however, it may give a more traditional feel. **Sans serif** fonts do not have serifs and tend to give a modern feel. They are easier to read on screen and can improve accessibility for dyslexic readers as they appear less cluttered. Facilities to **magnify** the screen or to change the font size displayed are also helpful.

Serif   Sans serif

'Sans' means 'without' in French.
'Sans serif' means 'Without serifs'.

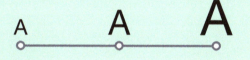

Colour schemes

Colour schemes should use contrasting text and backgrounds. Dark text on a light background is easiest to read, however, white text on a black background can also be very effective. **Colour blindness** can cause colours of a similar tone to look alike so greens and blues used together in a colour scheme, for example, would be difficult for some to tell apart.

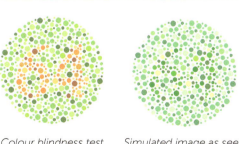

Colour blindness test   Simulated image as seen by a colour-blind person

Alt text

Alt text should be added to images and video. **Screen readers** or **text-to-speech** readers use this to inform a blind or partially sighted user of what media is showing. Text-to-speech also allows users to listen to a page of text.

Buttons

Navigation buttons should be clear and in **consistent positions** on each page of a web site or on each software screen. Large buttons can also help those who find mouse accuracy difficult.

Give **two** accessibility features used by supermarket self-checkouts to assist users.   [1]

A beep is heard when each item is scanned[1]. Instructions on the screen are also played in audio.[1] Specialised or tactile keypads.[1] High colour contrast on the display screen.[1]

IMPACTS OF MODERN TECHNOLOGIES ON ORGANISATIONS

Modern technologies have made many improvements for organisations and customers, but they also bring with them a variety of issues which need to be considered.

24/7 access, remote working and inclusivity

- Customers can access technologies, websites and telephone support any time of day or night.

- Staff may work more productively in a home environment and may take fewer days off sick.

- Less office space is required for remote employees which lowers rent and other overhead costs.

- If the company has 24/7 access, staff may be able to work more flexibly around their personal circumstances such as childcare or family members with disabilities.

- Staff can be employed from anywhere, not just locally. This can create a more inclusive work environment as people from different countries create a multicultural workplace.

- Remote working removes the need to commute. This means that a company can employ more people with physical or mental health conditions. For instance, someone who is agoraphobic (has a fear of open or crowded places) may find working from home easier than in an office.

- Computer systems need to have consideration for the additional needs that people may have. For instance, they allow text to be resized for those who have poor eyesight. Voice Assistants such as Amazon's Echo and Apple's Siri allow use without the need to type.

- Remote workers will each need additional devices such as printers as these cannot be shared.

- If a remote worker loses their Internet connection, they may be unable to continue their work or communicate with their colleagues.

- 24/7 access may encourage staff to work longer hours or feel unable to disconnect from work.

- Staff at home can be harder to manage remotely.

1. Explain **one** benefit to a bank when customers use Internet banking. [2]

Customers can use the service 24/7[1] so the bank can attract customers who cannot go to the bank branch during opening hours[1]. The customer can make bank transfers themselves[1] which gives more time for bank staff to work on other tasks[1].

Collaboration

- ⊕ Collaboration tools, such as wikis and blogs improve the speed of developing websites.
- ⊕ Many users are able to remove errors and make improvements as soon as they see them.
- ⊖ A user can deface a website or add information to a website that is factually untrue – this is especially a problem with wikis that have little restriction on the users that can update them.
- ⊖ It can be harder to control projects where everyone has access to make edits.

Accessibility

- ⊕ Modern technologies have vastly improved the quality and accessibility of devices and user interfaces. For instance, a modern tablet is far easier to use than an old text-based PC.
- ⊕ Operating systems, websites and software must have features to make them accessible to people with disabilities. Features include, changing text size, voice inputs and text to speech.
- ⊕ Companies need to make provision for a variety of different accessibility needs. For example, adding braille to an ATM cash machine makes it more accessible for the visually impaired.
- ⊕ Wearable technologies allow people to access their messages or health apps at any time.
- ⊕ Organisations must make technology accessible as part of the Equality Act (2010).
- ⊖ Wearable devices can collect very personal data such as medical information and location details – some will be uncomfortable with this.
- ⊖ Any personal data collected by smartphones and wearable devices will need to be stored securely in line with the Data Protection Act (1998).

Security of distributed/dispersed data

- ⊕ If copies of data are stored in many locations then the data won't be lost if there is a fire or flood in one location.
- ⊕ If small parts of data are distributed across different locations, and a criminal gains access to one server, they won't have access to all the data owned by the organisation.
- ⊕ Content delivery networks (CDNs) disperse copies of the same photos and videos in many data centres around the world. This allows website users to get data from servers nearer to them.
- ⊖ Having many copies of data stored in different locations means that some copies of the data may not be updated. This will lead to inconsistencies.

Distributed data is data that has been split into separate blocks and then stored in different locations.

Dispersed data means that many copies of the same data are stored in different locations.

2. A large multi-national car manufacturer may have car designs located in Japan, manufacturing located in the UK and sales information located France.
   Explain **one** disadvantage of data being distributed across many locations. [2]

It may take longer to access data[1] as if one country's server goes offline they may need to wait until the people managing it get it back online[1]. Each of the locations will need to be kept secure[1] which may increase the costs of storing data.[1]

IMPACTS OF MODERN TECHNOLOGIES ON INFRASTRUCTURE

Whilst modern technologies have many positive features, their impact on infrastructure requires careful management.

Required infrastructure

Infrastructure refers to the hardware and software systems, cloud services and general supplies that enable an organisation to run smoothly. The installation and maintenance costs of new infrastructure needs to be justified by increased future benefit or profits.

	Positive impacts	Negative impacts
Communication technologies	Communications technology improves collaborative working and increases the channels through which customers are able to contact an organisation.	Increased communications aren't always a constructive use of time. For instance, workers may find they are constantly interrupted by email, chats and text messages. If people don't have face to face contact they may feel more lonely or isolated.
Devices	Personal devices for each employee may provide greater flexibility of working.	Devices are expensive, have smaller screens than desktop displays and can be more easily damaged.
Local and web-based platforms	Local platforms keep control of security and data in-house. Web based platforms are accessible from anywhere and can improve collaborative working.	Web based platforms cannot operate without a good Internet connection. Local platforms require an in-house technical support team which may be more expensive.
Demand on, and availability of infrastructure	Cloud-based software can usually make use of existing computers and Internet connections. This saves companies the cost of buying new equipment.	A greater reliance on any network infrastructure will create greater issues when it fails to work. Training on how to use various platforms may also be required. A new cloud service may require an Internet connection with more bandwidth to be installed.

A call centre uses a local platform to answer customer calls and take notes. They will be moving to a web-based platform.

Explain **one** impact on their infrastructure as a result of this change. [2]

The web-based platform will make significant use of the Internet connection[1] which may result in all services that use the connection being slower.[1] The software won't make use of the local server[1] so this can be redeployed[1].

IMPACTS OF MODERN TECHNOLOGIES ON INDIVIDUALS

Modern technologies have transformed the way that people work in organisations.

 Early starts or commutes could be a thing of the past for remote workers, saving valuable time and shortening the working day. This creates more time for family or leisure.

 Flexible working means that staff can have schedules that best suit their lifestyle and family life. They can also work late at night or early in the morning if they prefer.

 Public transport or fuel costs would be greatly reduced without a regular commute. This would also benefit the environment.

 Home may be a less stressful working environment with greater control over the daily schedule leading to greater job satisfaction.

Explain how a poor Internet connection at home may affect access to home working opportunities or arrangements. [2]

A poor Internet connection will mean you have fewer job opportunities with companies offering home working only[1]. You may not be able to access job advertisements from companies who advertise online only[1]. If you are able to secure a job, you may find video conferencing difficult [1] and be unable to synchronise your files with the rest of the company in real time[1]. This may create delays and frustration[1].

 Access to a wider range of opportunities may be available to the less able or those who live very remotely.

 Staff can move about during the day, switching from one device to another depending on which is most suitable for their location. This may include **working from home**, or **remote working** at other offices, customer locations, coffee shops or on trips.

CASE STUDY

Think Impact Productions make dramas and documentaries for TV. They have around 20 employees that work in an office in Manchester. Many of their staff have started to ask if they can work from home. As a company that prides itself on 'putting people first', Think Impact will be allowing employees to work from home.

Evaluate the effect on individual well-being of employees being able to work from home. **[12]**

Benefits of remote working

- There will be **fewer distractions from other employees** which will **improve productivity** and sense of achievement – this could lead to a greater self-confidence of staff.
- Staff will find it easier to adjust their **schedule** of work to meet the **needs of their family**. They will then feel a greater **sense of control** over their schedule and work.
- Offices can be stressful environments, **working at home** can therefore **reduce stress**.
- They will spend **less time commuting**, so may find it easier to complete projects by deadlines, or may have **more time for their family** or interests.

Drawbacks of remote working

- If employees are working at home they won't find it as easy to bounce ideas off colleagues.
- They may be **responsible** for managing their own equipment. For example, if their Internet goes down then they will need to manage solving this problem.
- They may find that it is **harder to motivate** themselves to carry out the work required – this in turn could lead to **more anxiety** when deadlines are due.
- Working from home often means very **little face to face contact** with others, which could result in **loneliness** and even lead to **depression** – the company will need to be wary of this.

Discussion

- It will depend on the individual circumstances of employees as to whether remote working is better or worse for their **mental wellbeing**. It may be **hard to separate work and home** life.
- Think Impact Productions should explain the risks to staff and put in place some **social interaction**.
- **Guidance** should be given to dealing with stress and motivation.

Conclusion

- Remote working can have a positive effect where companies **support staff** in the transition.

Long answers must be written in paragraphs. Bullet points have been used here to make the answers easier to understand. This type of question will be marked using a Levels Based Marks Scheme. See page 76 for details.

EXAMINATION PRACTICE

Walter's Watersports is a water-based activity centre in the Lake District. The business is owned by Walter and they provide activities for groups of children and teenagers in the summer months. In the winter months they run adventure trips for adults abroad.

(a) Walter makes use of a website to capture information about schools that want to have activity days at the centre.

Annotate the form below to show **four** improvements that could be made to make it more accessible and user friendly. [4]

School activity enquiry

School name:

Teacher name:

Date for activity day:

Number of students:

Have you been before? | Submit |

(b) Walter's Watersports makes use of communication platforms such as their website and email to give information and communicate with customers.

Give **two** other communication platforms that they could use. [2]

Walter's Watersports communicates with stakeholders using their website.

(c) State **two** types of stakeholders that they may use the website to communicate with. [2]

(d) Walter wants to create a new page on his website that will advertise a new kayaking day that will appeal to teenagers.

Explain **two** ways that media could be used on this website. [4]

(e) Walter is concerned by negative effects that modern technologies are having on young people. He wants to build a page on his website that outlines some of the negative impacts of modern technologies that people could escape if they have a day at Walter's Watersports.

State **three** negative impacts that people may avoid by having a day at Walter's Watersports. [3]

(f) Walter uses a number of instructors to take water sports sessions. When they are not running activity days, they may be doing admin tasks or making training resources at home.

Explain **two** ways that scheduling and planning tools can help Walter manage his team of instructors. [4]

(g) State **one** collaboration tool that Walter may use with his instructors. [1]

WHY SYSTEMS ARE ATTACKED

Computer systems may be attacked for a number of reasons. As organisations become more reliant on these systems, more care needs to be taken to understand and block these threats.

Fun and challenge

Jack, 14, was woken at 08:10 one morning by a police riot van, a tech team and five police cars to arrest him.
He had stolen the personal details of 1000 people online in an exercise to prove to himself that 'he could do it'.

Personal attack

In 2008, Terry Childs was a network administrator for city of San Francisco in the USA. He was disgruntled with his employers, so locked access to their fibre network for 10 days by resetting the administrator passwords to all switches and routers. He received a five year prison sentence.

Financial gain

In 2017, WannaCry, a ransomware attack targeted Microsoft Windows users by encrypting their data and asking for ransom money to unencrypt it again for the victim. It is known that this alone earned hackers at least £108,000 in Bitcoin.

Industrial espionage

BAE systems is an aerospace company that discovered that their files had been compromised by a group aiming to steal their ideas and future strategic plans.

Data theft

In 2018, British Airways had over 300,000 customer credit card details stolen by online attackers. This data was then sold on the dark web to other cybercriminals who could use that data for personal phishing attacks.

Identify **two** ways in which an employee could accidentally cause a cyber security attack on their organisation. [2]

Falling victim to social engineering[1], someone shoulder surfing as they are entering a password[1], phishing scams[1], clicking on a suspect link in an email[1], failure to encrypt personal information[1], using an unsecured Wi-Fi connection.[1]

Disruption

The NHS suffered an attack in 2017 that diverted ambulances and cancelled operations causing huge disruption with the service.

INTERNAL THREATS TO DIGITAL SYSTEMS AND DATA SECURITY

There are many ways in which computer systems and data can be made vulnerable by people inside an organisation. Staff training and company policies can reduce the threat.

Unintentional disclosure of data
An employee may accidentally send information to a customer or member of the public.
For instance, they could attach the wrong file to an email.

Use of portable storage devices
Removable media, such as portable hard drives and USB flash drives, may contain viruses. When run on a company computer they may infect the network.

Users overriding security controls
Some users may be able to bypass existing security procedures in order to gain access to files that they should not see or run programs that they don't have permission to run. They may then leak or sell files that they gain.

Downloads from the Internet
Any files or programs that are downloaded from an untrustworthy source may contain malware. As a precaution all downloads should be scanned by anti-virus software before they are used on a system.

Intentional stealing or leaking of information
Dishonest or disgruntled employees may deliberately steal information for sale to other companies or hackers.

Visiting untrustworthy websites
Staff may visit questionable websites that may contain links to malware which could then be installed onto an organisation's computer or network. Phishing emails may also contain malware links so staff should be trained to spot these.

Explain how removable storage devices can cause harm to an organisation's computers or data.   [2]

The device could contain a virus[1] which would infect the computer when inserted to the computer[1].

USB devices can be deliberately infected with malware and left nearby a target organisation[1] in the hope that an employee will pick it up and use it within the company[1].

Portable devices can easily be lost or stolen[1] and may contain sensitive or confidential data[1].

EXTERNAL THREATS TO DIGITAL SYSTEMS AND DATA SECURITY

Hacking is unauthorised access to a computer system, program or data. A **black-hat** hacker has unethical, or malicious intentions. A rigorous security policy and set of procedures will reduce, but may not eliminate, the threat of attack.

Forms of attack and defence

Hacking
Brute-force attacks

Automated or manual attempts to gain unauthorised access to secure areas by trying all possible password or key combinations.

Strong passwords with limited attempts / Penetration testing ✔

Hacking
Denial of service (DoS) attacks

Servers and devices are flooded with too many requests or packets, causing them to crash or become unusable.

Firewall ✔

Botnet

Short for ro**bot net**work, a hacker will infect a zombie device which they can anonymously control to send spam, for DoS attacks or to mine cryptocurrency.

Firewall / Up-to-date virus checker ✔

Shoulder surfing

Looking over someone's shoulder when they enter a password or PIN.

Concealing your password or PIN entry / Privacy screens / User awareness ✔

Pharming

Cybercriminals install malicious code on your computer designed to redirect website traffic intended for one site, to a fake, official-looking website.

This can be used to harvest personal details from unsuspecting visitors.

Up-to-date virus checker ✔

Hacking
Man-in-the-middle attack (MITM)

An attacker intercepts communication between the user and server to eavesdrop or alter information.

Encryption ✔

Social engineering
Phishing

Phishing emails or texts redirect a user to a fake website where they trick the reader into divulging confidential information such as passwords that can be used fraudulently. Phishing phone calls can be used to obtain personal information or passwords.

User awareness of phishing 'clues' / Firewall ✔

Malware

Virus
A virus infects a host file and replicates itself on other computers. It causes damage to, or deletes software or data.

Trojans
A Trojan is code that is hidden inside an otherwise attractive program or utility that a user may want to download or install. When it runs it carries out malicious activity such as installing spyware or a rootkit.

Spyware
Hidden software that records keystrokes, passwords and other sensitive information to send back to a third party.

Worms
A worm is a program that will replicate itself and use up system or network resources.

Rootkit
Root access to a computer means administrator access. A rootkit allows a hacker to run any programs or see any files available on a computer.

Ransomeware
Ransomware holds a computer hostage by encrypting all data on the hard drive. The only way to read the data is to pay a ransom fee for the password that will decrypt the drive.

Cavendish Solicitors have just heard that they have suffered a major cyber-attack. Their IT manager says that a Trojan was used to install a rootkit on their server.

(a) Describe how a Trojan can be used to install other software. [3]

(b) State **two** capabilities that a rootkit could give a hacker. [2]

(a) A Trojan is hidden inside software that the users wants[1] which is first downloaded and installed[1]. When the software is installed, it also installs the Trojan horse[1] which will contain malware – in this case a rootkit[1].

(b) Run programs[1], copy/view files[1], change settings/passwords[1], create new accounts.[1]

IMPACTS OF A SECURITY BREACH

An organisation may face considerable difficulties or closure in the case of a breach in its security.

Reduction in productivity

A breach in security may make a system far slower. Data may need to be recovered from backups. This reduces how much work employees are able to do. The reduction in productivity will lead to lower profits or even losses for the company.

Financial loss

Putting right a breach can have a significant cost. The time lost fixing the situation also has a cost. An organisation may also incur substantial **fines** for a loss of personal data from the Information Commissioner's Office if they are found to have broken the **Data Protection Act**.

Any sensitive information about an organisation's future strategic plans may be leaked causing a loss of **competitive advantage** and future sales.

Data loss

A company's data is commonly considered to be its greatest asset. If records of customers, suppliers, sales or digital products are lost, few companies would be able to survive.

Downtime

Downtime is the amount of time that a computer, server or network isn't working. If a webserver is down, there may be a **loss of sales** from a website.

Damage to public image

If customers or suppliers are impacted by a breach of an organisation's security, their **reputation** may be severely affected. A loss of trust may result in a substantial loss of future business.

Legal action

Customers or suppliers whose data may have been compromised may have a right to **sue**. If there has been a breach of the Data Protection Act, the company may be fined.

KBS is an online bicycle parts specialist, selling to customers across the UK and Europe.

Discuss the impact on its stakeholders of their customer data being accessed by a hacker. [6]

A breach of customer data would be a breach of their duty to keep the data safe and secure[✓] under the Data Protection Act[✓]. They may need to pay a fine[✓] to the Information Commissioner's Office[✓]. The loss would be an embarrassment to the company and damage their public image[✓]. This would result in lower sales and add to their financial loss[✓]. The customers may experience stress or anxiety as a result of their information being compromised[✓]. If the hacker sells on the data, it may be used for identity theft[✓] which could be used by criminals to set up bank accounts and take out loans[✓]. Resolving this may cause customers a lot of effort and hardship[✓]. If credit card data was lost, customers may have transactions/theft that they need to resolve with their bank[✓]. The bank may make a loss in refunding these[✓] and they will also become less profitable as they will need to cancel their card and issue a new one[✓]. If the company suffers a large enough financial loss then they may go bankrupt[✓]. This will lead to employees losing their jobs, which could also be a significant impact on their families[✓].

CASE STUDY

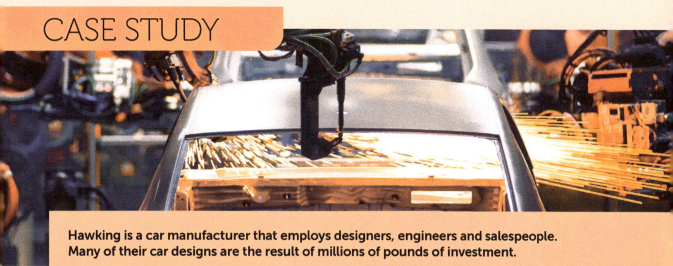

Hawking is a car manufacturer that employs designers, engineers and salespeople. Many of their car designs are the result of millions of pounds of investment.

Discuss the internal threats to their digital systems and data security, and the impact of a security breach. [6]

- There could be an **unintentional disclosure of data**. For example, a sales agent could attach the wrong quote to an email. This would result in a customer being able to see the price that a different customer pays. This would result in a **loss of reputation** with the company. If there is personal or confidential information on the quote, **legal action** may be taken against them

- An engineer will have access to the designs for the cars. There would be a considerable value to this **intellectual property**. They may be involved in **industrial espionage** and intentionally **steal this information** and give it to a competing car manufacturer.

- Engineers will have access to passwords for systems such as the robots that manufacture the cars. They may have a **personal issue** with the company and decide to create **disruption** to the assembly line. They could **override security controls** which will lead to damage to machinery or downtime.

- A designer may visit an **untrustworthy website** to **download** some specialist design software. The software could contain a Trojan horse – so whilst it installs and runs, it contains a **negative payload**. The negative payload could contain **spyware** that contains a **keylogger**. This would be able to log all passwords entered and send them to a **hacker** who could gain access to the computer network. The hacker could cause **data loss** by **deleting files** or release **confidential documents** resulting in damage to Hawking's **public image**. The hacker may have created **back doors** so they can enter the system again. Finding and removing these will lead to a **financial loss** for Hawking and it may also lead to a **reduction in productivity**.

- A salesperson may make use of a **portable storage device** to take customer information home so that they can continue sales calls. On the train home, they could lose the device. This would lead to a member of the public being able to open all the files and see all the confidential information. There could be damage to the company's public image. The **Information Commissioner's Office** would need to be informed of the **data loss**. There may be a fine and customers may take legal action against Hawking.

- A designer could have a virus on their home computer. They could do some work on this computer and then save it to a **USB flash media**. If they then took this into work the virus could infect their work computer and other computers on the network. This could lead to data loss, downtime and a reduction in productivity. All of these could lead to a significant financial loss for the company.

Long answers must be written in paragraphs. Bullet points have been used here to make the answers easier to understand. This type of question will be marked using a Levels Based Marks Scheme. See page 76 for details.

EXAMINATION PRACTICE

Muhammad works for Sekur Systems. They run cyber awareness training days for companies to explain about cyber security risks.

    (a) Two of the topics that they cover in their training are viruses and ransomware.

         Give **three** other types of malware that they may decide to cover.   [3]

    (b) Explain how a virus works.   [2]

    (c) Describe how ransomware works.   [3]

Eleanor has found a removable USB storage device in the car park. They are pleased as they recently lost their own company storage device which contained all their customer's details.

    (d) Describe the risk to Sekur Systems of Eleanor using the removable USB storage device which they found.   [2]

    (e) Eleanor has received an email from her boss saying that they need to discuss the serious impact of losing her storage device that contained customer's details.

         Explain **two** impacts to the organisation that may occur as a result of her losing the device.   [4]

    (f) Sekur Systems have been asked by one company to train their receptionists. The first training session will cover shoulder surfing.

         Explain why shoulder surfing would be a significant risk as a receptionist.   [2]

The second training for receptionists will cover both social engineering and phishing.

    (g) One method that a phishing attempt can be made is via email.

         State **one** alternative phishing method that could be used.   [1]

    (h) Describe how a phishing attempt could be made on a receptionist's email account.   [3]

Muhammad needs a slide for his presentation which will show how a man-in-the-middle attack could happen to someone who is working remotely in a café.

    (i) Annotate the diagram below to show how a man-in-the-middle attack could be carried out on someone working on their laptop and using a café's Wi-Fi.   [3]

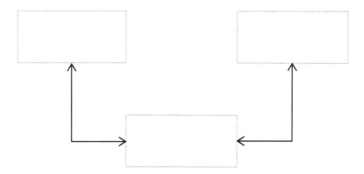

USER ACCESS RESTRICTION

There are various methods that can be used to reduce cyber-security threats. One is to reduce the number of people who have access to data and the volume of data they can access.

Physical security

Locks on doors to server rooms and data centres provide a good physical barrier. Other measures include **keypads**, **RFID** (**radio frequency ID**) card or **fob entry** systems and **security guards**.

Passwords

Usernames and **passwords** provide a first line of software defence for the opportunist hacker. A strong password can significantly hinder the progress of anyone attempting to access data.

Using the correct settings and levels of permitted access

Access levels restrict who can view, edit or delete files once they are logged in to an organisation's system. They may also restrict the programs that can be run. Ensuring these access levels are kept to a minimum for the job any individual is doing helps to narrow any risk.

Two-factor authentication

Authentication of an individual is used to make sure that a person is who they say they are. Two factor authentication asks questions of you based on any two from 'who you are', 'what you know' and 'what you have'. For example, a bank machine requires you to have a bank card (something you have) and to enter a PIN (something you know). A smartphone that just asks for a fingerprint uses only one-factor authentication (something you are).

Biometrics

Biometrics authenticate your body measurements as being uniquely yours. Methods include:

- Retinal scanning
- Iris recognition
- Face recognition
- Hand geometry / palm recognition
- Fingerprint recognition

Explain **one** reason why biometrics are effective for restricting user access. [2]

Verification is often faster than non-biometric methods[1] which means people are less frustrated/more efficient[1]. It is difficult to replicate or forge these features to fool systems[1] meaning that the person authenticated is likely to be who they say they are[1]. They can't be forgotten or written down, unlike passwords[1] so they won't be lost or disclosed[1].

DATA LEVEL PROTECTION

Device hardening

Device hardening is the practice of making devices harder to attack. Methods to do this include patching software vulnerabilities and tightly configuring user access levels. It also involves disabling unused network ports and non-essential services. In addition to this, alternative software such as **anti-virus** software can be used to reduce the level of threat posed by viruses.

Firewall

A **firewall** is **software** or a **hardware** device that monitors all incoming and outgoing network traffic. Using a set of rules, it decides whether to block or allow specific data packets such as those coming from a particular IP (Internet Protocol) address. Different services operate on different ports which can be blocked by a firewall. For example, web servers use port 80. If a server doesn't need to serve web pages, the port can be blocked preventing it being hacked.

Software interface design

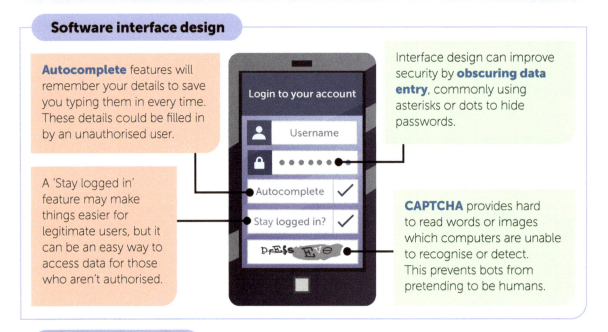

Autocomplete features will remember your details to save you typing them in every time. These details could be filled in by an unauthorised user.

A 'Stay logged in' feature may make things easier for legitimate users, but it can be an easy way to access data for those who aren't authorised.

Interface design can improve security by **obscuring data entry**, commonly using asterisks or dots to hide passwords.

CAPTCHA provides hard to read words or images which computers are unable to recognise or detect. This prevents bots from pretending to be humans.

Anti-virus software

Anti-virus software works by checking data against a database of **virus definitions**. It is important that this database is regularly **updated** to recognise and prevent the most recent threats. All external files should be scanned before use on internal networks within an organisation.

Backup and recovery procedures

An organisation must consider how, how often and where to back up their data. Once backed up, they also need to have policies in place that outline what to do and how to recover data should it become lost, stolen or damaged. See disaster recovery on Page 42.

ENCRYPTION

Encryption is the process of encoding data so that it cannot be easily understood if it is discovered, stolen or intercepted.

Encryption of stored data

It is possible to encrypt hard drives on a computer or storage for a smartphone or tablet. When the computer is turned on, a password is entered which allows the storage data to be **decrypted** and read. If a hacker removes the drive from the computer, they won't be able to read it as they won't have the **encryption key**.

As phones, tablets and computers contain personal and confidential information, it is important that they are encrypted. Backups also need to be encrypted in case they are stolen.

Decrypted

Confidential business meeting.

This document lays out the company's plans for a new...

Encrypted

Encryption of transmitted data

When data is sent through a network it is vulnerable to being read by an eavesdropper. When you visit a website using **HTTPS** (**Hypertext Transfer Protocol Secure**), the connection between your computer and the server is encrypted. The web address will show a padlock. No one else on the Internet will be able to read the communications. The website will send a digital certificate to the browser which the user can read to confirm the identity of the website.

Explain **one** reason why many businesses need to encrypt stored data. [2]

If any devices belonging to employees are lost or stolen[1] no one would be able to understand the data stored on the devices[1] unless they had the password to decrypt the information.[1]

Jfdu84N#*£sdDFLJML*&£83yfxc94

FINDING WEAKNESSES AND IMPROVING SYSTEM SECURITY

Cyber security professionals can be employed by companies to try and break into their systems.

Ethical hacking

Black hat hackers are criminals who break into computer systems without authorisation. They commonly have malicious intentions and are motivated by personal gain.

White hat hackers have permission to try and find weaknesses in a company's systems. They operate within ethical and moral boundaries. When weaknesses are found they report these back to the business so that the problems can be fixed.

Grey hat hackers operate in between. They typically have no malicious intent but do not always obtain permission from the system owners before trying to find weaknesses. If a vulnerability is found, they will often let the organisation know and may offer to fix it for a fee.

> Explain the difference between a white hat and grey hat hacker. [2]
>
> *A white hat hacker will be asked by a company to try to break into a computer system / run a penetration test (their hacking is legal)[1]. A grey hat hacker will not have permission to hack the system (and may be breaking the law)[1].*

System data analysis

Computers and servers can store logs of activity on computers. For instance, they may log attempts of users to log in to the system or which users opened, edited or deleted files. It is possible for both humans and computer programs to analyse this data for abnormal activity. This can identify potential risks or breaches before they happen. For example, they may notice lots of login attempts for one username. Or the logs may show that lots of files are being transferred by one user. This could be used to identify an account that is being used for industrial espionage.

Penetration testing

Penetration testing, or pen testing, is used to find weaknesses in a system by employing someone to break in. These vulnerabilities can then be fixed before a hacker has an opportunity to discover and exploit them.

CASE STUDY

Arabella is a wedding and portrait photographer. She shoots wedding photos on location and portraits of families in her home studio. Many of the photos she takes are irreplaceable life memories. Currently, Arabella makes no backups of her photos. Another photographer has said that this is very risky, so she is now considering her procedures for backing up and recovering data.

Discuss a suitable backup and recovery procedure for her photos. [6]

- The **SD card / removable media** in Arabella's **digital camera** could fail and lose all the photos on it. She should change this frequently throughout any shoots so that if the card fails only some of the photos will be lost. This **distributes** the data across a number of memory cards.
- Some cameras will allow two cards to be put in them at the same time. They can then be set to make an instant **backup** as each photo is taken.
- The cards will hold personal data. As such, Arabella will need to make sure they are stored securely to be **compliant** with the **Data Protection Act**.
- When on location, Arabella should store her cards in a locked bag somewhere **secure**. This will create a physical security measure. She will then need to make a further **backup copy** of the image data.
- When back in the studio Arabella can store the cards in a **fireproof locked safe**.
- At this stage, Arabella will need to **transfer** her photos to her computer for **editing**.
- The **backups** could be made on a second portable hard drive. If she uses a portable hard drive, she should make sure that this is stored securely at a remote location – that way if there is a fire or flood, the backup won't be lost.
- Arabella may wish to consider **backing up to the cloud**. This will mean the data is stored remotely so can be **accessed from anywhere**. The cloud provider will be responsible for making further backups which will save her time.
- By using a cloud provider, she will need an Internet connection to access her backups. It may also take a long time to backup and recover her photos without a fast, reliable connection.
- Arabella will need to consider how **frequently** she **makes backups**. She may choose to do this daily or after each photo shoot.
- As the data being stored is personal, Arabella will need to make sure that her editing computer and backups are **encrypted**. This will prevent people being able to see the photos if they steal the drives.
- Once Arabella has created her **backup procedure**, she needs to **test** it to see that she can successfully recover her photos.

Long answers must be written in paragraphs. Bullet points have been used here to make the answers easier to understand. This type of question will be marked using a Levels Based Marks Scheme. See page 76 for details.

EXAMINATION PRACTICE

Kingfisher bank is a new bank that is fully digital. They have no branches and only operate via their website and an app.

At head office, all users must use a password to log onto their computer.

(a) Give **two** physical security measures that could be used to restrict access to the computers. [2]

(b) In two-factor authentication, one possible factor is 'something the person is', for example, their fingerprints or face.

Give an example for each of the following factors:

- 'Something you know'. [1]
- 'Something you have'. [1]

(c) The bank will make use of two-factor authentication every time someone wishes to use their app to send money.

Describe how they could achieve this. [2]

(d) The computers located inside the bank's head office need to be protected from attacks via their Internet connection. One way they do this is by making use of a hardware firewall.

Annotate the diagram below to show how a hardware firewall works. [4]

(e) The bank undergoes penetration testing once a year.

Describe how penetration testing will be used to improve the bank's security. [3]

(f) When a customer visits the bank's website it will always use an encrypted connection.

Describe how a user can check that they are transmitting data in a secure and encrypted way with the bank's website. [2]

DEFINING RESPONSIBILITIES

Security policies set out how people and systems should act in certain situations. They show who is responsible for actions, what they should do and when they should do it. Without the implementation of clear policies, cyber-security issues are more likely to occur and may quickly escalate to have serious implications.

Who is responsible for what?

People take on different responsibilities. For example, a **data protection officer** will check that personal data is protected, whilst a **network manager** will be responsible for **network security**.

How do I report a concern?

Most companies invite employees to raise concerns without fear of dismissal or discrimination for speaking out. By having clear **responsibilities**, employees know which person to go to.

How will staff know what to do?

Staff will be trained in certain key cyber-security risks. Staff will also be expected to read policies such as the **Acceptable Use Policy** before being given access to computers. Managers will frequently update staff with new risks and methods of attack so that they can be vigilant.

DEFINING SECURITY PARAMETERS

Organisations will have a number of policies that cover cyber-security and the use of computers. Some key policies and example contents are shown below.

Password policy

1. Ensure that all passwords are strong, by including at least eight characters with a mixture of uppercase and lowercase letters, symbols and numbers.
2. Do not include personal information e.g. DOB.
3. Change passwords regularly.
4. Keep passwords secure and never write them down.

Acceptable usage policy

Contents:
1. Appropriate behaviour using computer systems.
2. Locking unattended computers.
3. Prohibited behaviour:
   i. Sending inappropriate communications.
   ii. Downloading or installing files and software.

Parameters for device hardening

Setup and configuration of systems.
   (a) Applying security patches.
   (b) Installation of antivirus software and firewalls.
   (c) Configuring security settings and user access.
   (d) Encryption of drives and backups

DISASTER RECOVERY POLICY

Disasters include fire, flood, earthquakes, and hurricanes. Well planned responses can dramatically improve the recovery times and level of success for an organisation hit by disaster.

The backup process

Backups need to be **scheduled** to meet the needs of a business. Each **full backup** needs a large amount of storage. If a business only opens Monday to Friday, there is no need to make further backups on Saturday and Sunday. A business will often make a full backup at the start of the week, then just make an **incremental backup** of new or updated files on the other days. This reduces the storage requirement.

Monday	Tuesday	Wednesday	Thursday	Friday	Saturday	Sunday
Full backup	Incremental backup	Incremental backup	Incremental backup	Incremental backup	No backup today	No backup today

Businesses will often backup their data to **tape drives** for storage **off-site.** This is cheap and **reliable**. They may alternatively backup to a **remote backup server** or **cloud based system**. Smaller organisations and freelancers may backup to a **portable hard disk** that they store at a **remote location**. This avoids purchasing an expensive tape drive. Some people will backup to **DVDs** or **Blu-rays** which are inexpensive, but need to be stored carefully to avoid scratches and direct sunlight.

File servers will often contain a second hard disk, known as a **mirror**, that provides an exact copy of the first. This is known as a **RAID (Redundant array of independent disks)**. When a file is saved it is stored on both disks. If one hard disk **fails**, it can be taken out and replaced with a new one whilst the server is still **running**. This avoids any **downtime** due to a broken hard disk.

Disaster recovery plans

In the event of a disaster causing a loss of data, premises or staff, an organisation must have comprehensive plans to recover the data from a backup and get computer systems up and running again. A **timeline** will be needed that shows the order that different systems are restored. The most important systems will be scheduled to restore first. In the event of an emergency, plans should be made for **alternative premises** or **home working**, and **alternative hardware suppliers** with the correct replacement stock available. The correct software will need to be reloaded onto each new computer. Plans will also need to be made to cover for **key personnel** who may leave the organisation at short notice.

Duties

Staff at all levels in the organisation need to be clear on what to do in the event of an cyber-attack or natural disaster. This may involve investigating logs or reports of irregular activity on a network, or following procedures given in the disaster policy.

1. A company is open Tuesday to Sunday each week. Describe a sensible backup schedule.[2]

   A schedule could make a full backup[1] every day except Monday[1]. It could make a full backup at the start of the week[1], then further incremental backups each day[1].

ACTIONS TO TAKE AFTER A DISASTER

The following five-stage plan is used to show the actions to take in the event of a disaster or cyber-attack.

1	2	3	4	5
Investigate the problem	Respond	Manage the issues	Recover	Analyse

1. **Investigate — Establish severity and nature:** An organisation needs to quickly establish the nature of the attack or problem, how damaging it has been and what systems have been affected. They may also examine how long the attack has been going on for.

2. **Respond — Inform and update stakeholders and authorities:** When an incident occurs, the correct people need to be informed. For instance, if customers' personal data is stolen, a network administrator may be involved in fixing a security hole, whilst the **data protection officer informs the authorities** (**Information Commissioner's Office**). A **customer services manager** may have to inform customers of the data loss.

3. **Manage — Containment procedures begin:** The attack or natural disaster should be contained. Systems may need to be shut down or disconnected.

4. **Recover — Implement disaster recovery plan:** Remedial action such as replacing damaged hardware, restoring backups or moving premises will now be carried out in line with the disaster recovery plan.

5. **Analyse — Update policy and procedures:** The incident will be studied to evaluate how well the policy and procedures worked and what lessons have been learnt. Policies will be updated to improve their effectiveness.

2. The five-step process of investigation, response, management, recovery and analysis is commonly adopted in disaster control.

Explain why the Analysis stage takes place at the end of the process. [2]

The whole incident can be reflected upon[1] with consideration to what parts of the existing disaster recovery policy worked and where it can be improved[1] before the policy is updated[1].

CASE STUDY

BMC Pharmaceuticals is a medical research company. They recently suffered a ransomware attack. An investigation was carried out which determined that one of the researchers in the company clicked an advertisement on a webpage which downloaded the malware. They then opened the file which caused the ransomware to encrypt the hard disk and infect other computers on the network.

Fortunately, the company had a robust disaster recovery plan and was able to restore all data and rebuild the computers within two days.

They are now analysing their acceptable use policy (AUP) and the parameters for device hardening.

Discuss updates that could be made to the policy which would help to prevent such an attack occurring again.   [6]

- It is most likely that files infected with **malware** were downloaded from a website that was not hosting legitimate information. The researcher may have arrived at the website by mistyping a web address or going to an **untrustworthy site**. As such, **training** should be provided to **staff**. The **AUP** should mention that staff must be responsible in the websites they choose to visit.

- The file that was downloaded should have been checked for **viruses**. **Anti-virus software** was probably already installed, however, it is important that the virus definitions are **updated** at least once a day. This will help to **harden devices**. This responsibility can be assigned to a systems manager.

- The researcher will probably have had the **permission** to run and **install software** in order to cause it to infect the computers. In most cases, staff can have this permission removed. Software installation can be carried out by the company's IT support. They will be more likely to notice suspicious software and may wish to run it on a test machine before putting it on a machine on the network. The AUP can be updated to let staff know that they do not have permission to install software.

- **Logs** can be taken of system activity. Alerts can be setup to inform systems administrators of irregular behaviour. In this case, encrypting a hard disk is very resource intensive. It may well be possible to detect that one or more hard disks are undergoing abnormally heavy usage. A quick investigation may reveal the problem and minimise the damage.

- The company was able to restore all computers within two days, however, they should look to whether this time could be reduced further. Perhaps they should have additional hardware ready in case this happens again. They should also consider how long it took to get backups restored. If **backups** are made to hard drives, are these quickly **accessible** whilst still being at a remote location?

- The company should consider the timeline for **data recovery**. Were the most important computer systems restored quickly? Could the order be altered to minimise disruption?

Long answers must be written in paragraphs. Bullet points have been used here to make the answers easier to understand. This type of question will be marked using a Levels Based Marks Scheme. See page 76 for details.

EXAMINATION PRACTICE

Alpha Heights is a European theme park. They have computer systems in their ticket booths and restaurant payment systems. They also have computers that control the rides. A small team of employees work on managing the park and marketing. Other employees are typically temporary and only work for six months of the year during the warmer months.

(a) Explain **two** features of a suitable password policy for temporary staff. [4]

(b) The acceptable use policy states that staff must lock their computer or log out of their computer if they are away from it for longer than 10 seconds. Some staff have suggested that this is unnecessary.

Explain why this rule may have been added to the acceptable use policy. [2]

(c) Other than a password policy, state **two** other measures that would help to harden devices. [2]

(d) Alpha Heights has a disaster recovery policy.

State **two** disasters that this is likely to cover. [2]

The disaster recovery policy for Alpha Heights covers the backups that will be made.

(e) To reduce the storage space required for each backup, certain files will not be backed up.

Explain **one** type of file that may not be backed up. [2]

(f) Name **three** types of media that could be used to make the backups. [3]

(g) One of the responsibilities that is defined in Alpha Heights' disaster recovery policy is the need to keep all personal data on their systems secure.

State **one** person in the organisation who may be responsible for this. [1]

(h) As part of Alpha Heights' disaster recovery policy, they have been very careful in considering the timeline for data recovery.

Describe a possible timeline for data recovery that Alpha Heights may have put into their disaster recovery policy. [3]

SHARING DATA RESPONSIBLY

Computer systems and services provided by the organisations who operate them share and exchange data in ways that affect their stakeholders.

A **digital footprint** is created whenever anyone interacts with a computer system. This could include bank machines, mobile phones, automatic number plate recognition or social media use.

Location based data

Global Positioning Systems (GPS) chips are embedded inside smartphones, satnav systems, electronic ankle tags and vehicles. These can be used to track the location of the user, car or package delivery for example.

Benefits to users	Drawbacks for users
Convenience in finding map directions, updates on expected deliveries, locating friends and family, tracking the spread of disease and for use with fitness apps.	Your location data can be shared with the police, advertisers looking for people in a particular area at a particular time or it could fall into the hands of criminals. GPS also consumes more battery power.

Transactional data

Each time an item is purchased, either online or inside a shop using a bank or store card, data about that purchase is stored and shared between the store and the card supplier. This may include where you are making the purchase, when, what you are buying, if you used a voucher, how you paid and any related loyalty card number. This shopping history is used to create a profile for you and compared to other purchase items you select and your shopping behaviours. Any transactional data must be collected appropriately, in agreement with the individual and in accordance with the law.

⊕ This can make shopping more personalised with offers on things shoppers are known to buy.

⊕ Data can be used to create a better shopping experience.

⊖ It can also be passed or sold on to other companies who may use it for unsolicited marketing.

⊖ The data could also be used in identity theft if it got into the wrong hands.

Website cookies

A **cookie** is a small file that is created on a user's computer when they visit a website. Cookies will record an ID number for the user so that they can be recognised the next time they visit the site. This allows a user to remain logged into a website when they next visit. Their personal account information such as previous purchases, layout, and interactions with content are conveniently saved for future sessions by the website. The website can also tailor content to the user when they next visit based on this information. Websites are legally required to get **consent** from users to use cookies when they first visit. Those who find this an invasion of their privacy are able to disable cookies, but this may stop the website functioning properly.

Explain **two** advantages to a website owner of using cookies. [2]

A website can use a cookie to remember a visitor to a website[1], this saves them having to log in the next time they visit[1]. Cookies can be used to track users as they browse a website[1] so that the web developer/site owner can build up a profile of similar behaviours across users[1].

Items placed in an online shopping basket can be saved for the customer's next visit[1] to save them time looking for them again.[1]

Sharing data

Data exchange between services makes online shopping and other online services possible. For example, credit card details may be shared between an online shop and a card provider. The exchange of data has both benefits and drawbacks.

Benefits	Drawbacks
Documents can be shared increasing opportunities for collaboration.	**Privacy** and **legal concerns** must be addressed.
Shared calendars allow automatic updating of events.	Data may not be used **ethically** – e.g. spam email.
Photos can easily be shared with family members.	Photos can easily be shared by others infringing on privacy.

Responsible use of data

Organisations are legally bound by the **Data Protection Act** to ensure that all data they collect is accurate, appropriate and not disclosed to others without their permission. Laws also govern the use of cookies. Organisation that use data unethically or illegally will suffer reputational damage and could be heavily fined.

ENVIRONMENTAL RESPONSIBILITIES

Use of IT systems

The use of computers systems and devices consumes a huge amount of **electricity**. Many servers and devices are left on **24/7**.

Manufacture of IT systems

The manufacture of computers and electronic devices commonly requires **rare earth metals**, **toxic chemicals** and **oil-based plastics**. **Mining**, **extraction** and **processing** of these materials requires huge amounts of **water** and **energy**, can scar the landscape and creates harmful **waste** materials. Components are sourced from all over the world, including countries where **health and safety** and **environmental protection standards** are not always as high as those in the UK.

Bean LLP is a legal firm who replace all of their computers on a three-year cycle.

Explain **one** advantage to the business and **one** disadvantage to the business of doing this. [4]

Advantages: Computers will be newer and this likely makes them faster which increases productivity[1]. They will be more energy efficient[1] which lowers electricity costs / decreases their carbon footprint[1].

Disadvantages: Costs of replacing computer hardware may be high[1] leading to lower profits[1]. The company are obliged to dispose of the e-waste properly[1] which may have a cost associated with it.[1]

Disposal of IT systems

Electronic waste (or **e-waste**) must be disposed of correctly in accordance with the **Waste Electrical and Equipment Regulations (WEEE) 2019** or using a legal disposal company to prevent waste going to landfill. Some nations accept e-waste for processing in their own countries, but this can often end up in waste heaps, leaking poisonous substances into the environment.

In 2019, there were an estimated 2 billion computers in use across the world including desktops, laptops and servers. There are a further 4.7 billion mobile phones — each of which may have been designed to fail after a given period. These will require manufacture, regular charging and careful disposal or recycling.

USAGE AND SETTINGS POLICIES

Individual and organisational policies can reduce the impact of technology on the environment.

Power saving settings

Most devices have power saving features to reduce their consumption of battery life or mains electricity. These can be set by individual users or for all users in a company.

Auto power off settings will switch off devices if they sense no input for a given length of time. This is sometimes referred to as **sleep mode**. Computers left on **standby** will still use power.

Power saving settings should be adjusted to the maximum level appropriate. Reducing **screen brightness** is a common example. This improves **battery life**.

Hard and soft copies

Printed (**hard**) copies of documents use paper which is manufactured from trees. Using and distributing documents electronically (**soft copies**), for commenting and reading on screen, reduces this impact. Some energy will still be used running computers and devices.

Upgrades, replacements, repairs and recycling

As computers get older, companies have two choices. They can replace the computer by purchasing a new one, or they can upgrade existing computers. Upgrading computers, by increasing the amount of RAM or the size of a hard drive, may be cheaper and have less environmental impact. When replacing computers, it is important that energy efficient replacements are purchased.

Some organisations may **recycle** equipment, especially consumables such as printer toner cartridges and paper. Recycling computer parts is not so straightforward. Materials are not always easy to separate from each other so careful consideration of use needs to be made.

Ensure that old hard drives are **wiped** before they are passed on to others for second-hand use, for recycling or for disposal. This removes all data including deleted files.

Tim has used a laptop device for a sales job over the past four years. The battery life has reduced to roughly one hour.

Describe **two** ways in which his battery life could be extended. [4]

Turn off Wi-Fi, Bluetooth or GPS features[1] as these consume background power[1]. Reduce screen brightness[1] so that the display uses less energy[1]. Close apps that are running in the background[1] to reduce processing power[1]. Install the latest updates[1] to improve efficiency[1]. Ensure that the power mode[1] is set to the most efficient setting[1].

CASE STUDY

BestNutrition Foods offer a home delivery service for groceries. Customers can order from them online using a smartphone app. They can then track the progress and location of the delivery as it moves through their system via the app.

Customer information is shared with other companies such as their delivery network and card processing company. The company also shares data such as the GPS location of the customer's delivery. BestNutrition shares customer information with similar companies that may wish to advertise to the customer.

Discuss the benefits and drawbacks of the company using shared data. Include in your response any legal, privacy or ethical considerations. [6]

- The customer enters their information such as address to BestNutrition. By sharing this information with the delivery network, they know where to deliver the items.

- The customer can **update** their **delivery details**. When this happens, both BestNutrition and the delivery company will have the correct details. This improves the **accuracy** of their **data** and is more efficient than the customer having to phone or write to the company with the updated details.

- BestNutrition gives the customer constant updates as to how their order is progressing and where their delivery is. This reduces the need for a customer to phone them to ask these questions and leads to **higher productivity**, higher profits, and better **customer satisfaction**.

- When **sharing customer information** with similar companies, BestNutrition will need to make sure they have the **consent** of the customer to do this. They will need to record this consent. If they don't do this, they will be in breach of the **Data Protection Act**.

- The customer may not fully understand how their data may be used. If BestNutrition have confusing materials, that aim to trick customers into sharing their personal data, this would be unethical and illegal.

- By sharing the **GPS coordinates** of the delivery van with the customer, the driver may find that they are under more pressure to deliver to a schedule. This could increase their **stress** or risk of a traffic accident.

- If personal data were stolen from BestNutrition, or any of the partners they share the information with, they could be fined by the **Information Commissioner**. They would also suffer damage to their **reputation**. They therefore need to carefully consider their **cyber security** measures such as **firewall** settings and user **password strength**.

- Information that is shared between companies should only be that which they require. For instance, to improve the **privacy** of drivers, the delivery company should not share their name with BestNutrition as the customer doesn't need to know this **personal information**.

Long answers must be written in paragraphs. Bullet points have been used here to make the answers easier to understand. This type of question will be marked using a Levels Based Marks Scheme. See page 76 for details.

EXAMINATION PRACTICE

Abigail runs a hair salon in Birmingham. She has a website where customers can make bookings and find out information about the services that she offers. Hair services are paid for by cash or card. In addition, other hair products sold in the shop can be purchased by card on the website.

(a) Name **four** items of transactional data that may be shared between the website and the staff in the hair salon when a customer makes a booking. [4]

In the past, a list of customer appointments used to be printed out at the start of each day and placed on a noticeboard in the salon. These details are no longer printed. Instead, they are accessed through a tablet.

(b) Explain **one** legal issue of having the customer appointments printed on a wall in the salon. [2]

(c) Describe **two** benefits of having the personal data only available on the tablet. [4]

Luna is a salon employee who will shortly be leaving the salon to start her own mobile hair business. She is considering sending the list of customers at the salon to her personal email address so that she can contact them later to see if they would like to have their hair done in their home.

(d) Explain **one** ethical reason why Luna should not do this. [2]

(e) Explain **one** legal reason why Luna should not do this. [2]

The tablet used by staff used to last all day when running on the battery. It now only lasts a couple of hours. This has made it harder for staff to use the tablet. Abigail has found that the battery is sealed in the tablet, so she will need to replace it.

(f) Explain **two** environmental impacts of replacing the tablet. [4]

The salon has a desktop computer in the office. Abigail has noticed recently that she has high electricity bills for the salon. A friend has said that her computer is probably one of the causes.

(g) Describe how Abigail could change the power-saving settings of her computer to reduce its energy usage. [3]

EQUAL ACCESS

The **digital divide** is a term used to describe the gap between those with access to digital services and information and those without. **Equal access** serves to narrow this gap.

Connectivity to the **Internet infrastructure** and the speed of this connection is a major factor in the levels of access people have. Other factors include age, IT skills, disabilities and poverty.

Computers per 100 people

- 0–5
- 5–13
- 13–25
- 25–50
- 50–89
- No data

Legal requirements

The **Equality Act 2010** requires employers not to **discriminate** people based on a **protected characteristic**. Examples of protected characteristics include age, disability, pregnancy, race, religion or sex. For instance, a website designer would need to make sure their website was accessible to a blind person as this is a disability.

Professional guidelines and accepted standards

The **British Computer Society (BCS)** offer a code of conduct to how their members must behave professionally. For instance, members can only carry out work which is within their skill level.

Web Content Accessibility Guidelines (WCAG) offer direction on how to optimise a website for **inclusivity**.

Assess the benefits of equal access to the Internet to organisations, individuals and society. As part of the assessment make a judgement on the importance of equal access. [9]

If a person has access to a high quality Internet connection and computer they will find it easier to gain employment[✓]. This is because they can educate themselves using video websites or online university materials[✓] or search for more jobs online[✓]. Some remote jobs, such as telesales, require a stable and reliable connection[✓]. Individuals will have a greater variety of jobs to choose from if they have a good Internet connection[✓]. Individuals frequently cite technology as being their link to the outside world socially[✓]. Without access, they may feel lonely and isolated.[✓] Online shopping can bring greater discounts than might otherwise be available on the high street.[✓] Other online services such as banking[✓] can also reduce the need to travel and improve life efficiencies[✓] saving both money and time[✓].

Organisations benefit from equal access since the potential workforce available will be greater[✓] and those already employed are better skilled at using computers[✓], and better informed of IT systems and working practices[✓]. They are also able to advertise and communicate to customers online[✓] which widens their reach[✓]. Employees who are proficient with IT are generally more productive[✓]. This provides the company with a greater competitive edge[✓] and greater sales revenue[✓].

Society benefits through additional taxation because individuals and companies benefit financially[✓]. Online government services can be made more efficient by reducing the need for call centres[✓]. Having good access to IT enables people to be more entrepreneurial[✓] which can result in the creation of jobs for others[✓].

Equal access provides significant benefits to individuals, organisations and society. As long as computers are used wisely and have a purpose[✓], equal access is an important societal aim.

This question should be marked with reference to the levels-based mark scheme on page 76.

C2

NET NEUTRALITY

Net neutrality says that all services and web content providers should be treated equally. This prevents an **Internet Service Provider (ISP)** from slowing down or blocking services such as Voice over Internet Protocol (VoIP) or giving greater bandwidth to one streaming video provider over another.

JUMP! is a new children's video streaming service. Explain **one** advantage to JUMP! of net neutrality. [2]

Net neutrality maintains the same Internet service quality to all customers/organisations[1]. As a small start-up company, JUMP! will get the same quality of service as a larger streaming service[1]. ISPs are not allowed to block JUMP!'s streaming service[1]. This enables JUMP! to fairly compete with larger companies[1].

ACCEPTABLE USE POLICIES

An **Acceptable Use Policy (AUP)** states the rules that staff need to adhere to with respect to the use of IT **assets** such as computer and network equipment, software, documents and knowledge in an organisation. The **scope** of the AUP shows exactly who it applies to. For instance, in a company it may just apply to the employees, whereas in a school it will also cover students.

The AUP explains which behaviours are **acceptable** and encouraged in the organisation and which are **unacceptable**. For example, it may state that people need to lock a computer when they are not near it, or that they must not write abusive emails.

All users of an organisation's IT systems will need to sign a document to **acknowledge** that they agree to abide by the AUP. The agreement will be acknowledged with a **signature**. Users may also need to **click to accept** the AUP each time they log on. The AUP will also define the processes and sanctions that will happen if unacceptable behaviour occurs.

Monitoring

Organisations may monitor user behaviour when using their IT network. This may include:

- Logs of which web pages have been accessed and searches that have been made.
- Incoming and outgoing calls and emails.
- Logs of every time a user logs on or off and what programs or files they access.

1. Give **three** items that may appear in an Acceptable Use Policy. [3]

Appropriate use of computer equipment[1]. Appropriate use of the Internet[1]. Use of own password only[1]. Rules on password strength[1]. Restrictions on which files or folders can be accessed[1]. The appropriate use of email and social media[1] including not sending spam[1] or writing a threatening/abusive email or post [1].

Did you sign an Acceptable Use Policy for the computer equipment at school? What was in the agreement?

2. An AUP commonly allows an organisation to monitor the activities of its members. This includes all communication content, computer logins and website access.

   Explain **one** advantage of this to the organisation. [4]

If important documents are deleted[1] it is possible to work out which user deleted them[1] and give an appropriate sanction[1]. If inappropriate websites are visited[1] these will be listed in the logs[1]. If an employee is accused of being abusive[1] their email can be checked to find evidence[1]. This can lead to disciplinary procedures[1]. As staff know that misconduct is monitored[1] they will receive less abuse through email[1] leading to a happier workplace[1].

SOCIAL AND BUSINESS BOUNDARIES

Social media has become widely used at home and in the workplace – often by the same people. This has blurred the lines between personal and working lives.

Social media

Social media provides a platform for organisations to communicate and engage with customers, frequently on a more informal basis.

Marketing – Organisations can post photo and video adverts online and track their response very accurately to gather market intelligence.

Communication – A new channel for questions and answers is opened up with existing and potential customers.

Awareness – A social media campaign is a useful tool for launching new ideas, movements and **branding**. It is also useful for maintaining awareness of an existing brand.

Recruitment – Some organisations use social media for advertising new positions within their company. Social media adverts may target specific **demographics**.

Influence – Social media **influencers** build brands by showcasing their goods or services in a positive light. This can be very lucrative for both the influencer and the brand.

Impact of personal use of social media and the web on professional life

Each time a user posts something on their social media profile, it is unlikely ever to be removed from the Internet and could become public, even if they have set their profile to private.

- Users who post negative, discriminatory or inflammatory comments or photos could have problems with their employer and even lose their job. Poor behaviour depicted in a profile will likely affect job opportunities or prospects if these can be publicly seen.

- Those who demonstrate excellent social media and communications skills online may find it helps them with employment.

DATA PROTECTION PRINCIPLES

The Data Protection Act 2018

The Data Protection Act aims to help protect and give people more control over their personal data. The data must be stored and processed according to the following principles:

1. Lawful processing
2. Collect only for specific purposes
3. Only collect the minimum information that is needed
4. Data must be accurate and kept up to date
5. Only keep data as long as is necessary
6. Keep data in accordance with data subjects' rights
7. Protect data with appropriate security methods
8. Do not transfer data to countries with less protection

Organisations seeking to collect personal data need to register with the Information Commissioner's Office (ICO), providing information about what data they collect, its purpose and who the **data protection officer** is.

Companies must have consent to legally use cookies

A person is known as a data subject. **Data subject rights** include:

- The right to view data stored about you by organisations
- The right to withdraw consent – this allows you to be removed from a mailing list
- The right to make changes to your data if it is inaccurate
- The right to be forgotten – this allows you to delete your personal data

ParcelChimp is a courier company. They require customers to register via their website with their personal information before sending a parcel.

(a) Give **two** ways in which the web form shown below can be amended to improve the accuracy and relevance of data collection. [2]

Parcel chimp makes use of transactional data as part of providing the delivery service, marketing and reporting their tax.

(b) Explain **one** legal consideration they need to make when handling transactional data. [2]

(a) Email address field could be validated to contain an @ symbol for the correct format.[1] Postcode fields could use a lookup for improved accuracy.[1] Marital status can be removed as it is not relevant.[1]

(b) As part of the data collection for the delivery service, they should explain to users how their data is used[1] and who they share it with / what data subject's rights are[1]. They must obtain consent[1] to use the data for marketing. Data subjects will be able to withdraw their consent if they wish. They do not need to obtain consent for processing data for tax purposes[1], however, they need to store this data securely using encryption[1]. Data breaches can result in fines up to 4% of ParcelChimp's turnover or up to €20 million.

DEALING WITH INTELLECTUAL PROPERTY

Intellectual property covers any assets which are not physical. These include logos which are protected by trademarks, inventions which can be patented and the copyright of books, photos, music, video and computer games.

Legal and ethical use of intellectual property (IP)

Ideas and assets protected by the **Copyright, Designs and Patents Act 1988** may be copied, modified or distributed by other companies provided they have conducted themselves appropriately and requested permissions through the correct channels. Individuals and companies can take legal action against anyone who uses their IP without permission.

Intellectual property is one of the most valuable assets of many organisations. Imagine the impact of to Coca-Cola of another drinks manufacturer using their recipe and logo.

Registered trademarks

Registered trademarks protect distinguishable brand logos, words and slogans. Examples include the Nike logo, the Facebook® name and the McDonalds® "I'm lovin' it®" slogan.

An organisation can agree to another company using their IP. This is known as **licensing**.

Patents

Patents are granted by the Intellectual Property Office (IPO) to protect inventions. Examples include Dyson® Cyclone vacuum cleaners and the Super Soaker toy design.

Until the patent has expired after 20 years, companies are prohibited from using these ideas in their own designs without a **licence** agreement.

Copyright

Copyright is automatically granted on original software and written musical, dramatic or artistic works.

Permission to use a copyrighted work will be needed from the copyright holder.
An acknowledgement or **attribution** of the original source may also be required.

FoldOut creates clever folding furniture designs.

(a) Describe the impact on their business if other companies or individuals began to copy their designs, without permission, to make their own cheaper versions of the furniture. [2]

(b) Explain **two** ways in which FoldOut could protect their intellectual property. [4]

(a) FoldOut may never recover the money they spent on researching and developing the design from sales[1] if sales are diverted to another company selling cheaper copies[1]. This may cause confusion in the market over who owns the designs[1], damage the FoldOut brand[1] or bankrupt them[1]

(b) They could register the trademark for the FoldOut name / logo[1] which would help protect it from others passing off their products / copying it[1]. The clever folding design invention could be patented[1] to give FoldOut an exclusive right to make or licence the invention[1]. Any images, photos or text that FoldOut has created would be protected automatically by copyright[1]. They should add © and the year of publication so that others are aware that it should not be copied.[1]

CRIMINAL USE OF COMPUTER SYSTEMS

Legislation has been created to prevent hacking and the distribution of malware.
Cybercrime refers to the use of computer systems to commit crime.

Computer Misuse Act 1990

The Computer Misuse Act was introduced in 1990 to make unauthorised access to programs or data (hacking) and cybercrime illegal. The law makes the following illegal:

- Unauthorised access to computer systems and data
- Unauthorised access to computer systems and data with a further criminal intent
- Unauthorised modification of computer materials.

The Police and Justice Act 2006

This Act makes it illegal to intend to impair the operation of a computer. This prevents hackers from creating or distributing malware or carrying out denial of service (DoS) attacks.

Convictions for these offences can carry a fine and up to 10 years imprisonment.

Atticus works for an Internet retailer. He has access to the company computers, but his account doesn't have the access rights to see the company finances. He watched his colleague in the finance department enter their password and intends to use their account to view the data.

(a) Explain how Atticus will be breaking the law if he logs in with a colleague's password. [1]

(b) Atticus has received an email that contains an attachment. Atticus knows that the attachment contains a virus. He decides to play a prank on a colleague by sending it to them. Explain how he has broken the law. [2]

(a) *He will be gaining unauthorised access to a computer system[1] which is illegal under the Computer Misuse Act[1].*

(b) *He has distributed malware[1] which is against the Police and Justice Act[1].*

CASE STUDY

Dance17 is a street dance academy for young people aged 11–17. They have launched several new dance groups with national and international competition success.

Aaron runs the academy in the evenings and at weekends. He has around 200 dancers which need to register when they join the academy. Parents also need to give their permission along with any relevant medical information about their child.

Discuss the data protection implications of Dance17 processing and storing personal information. As part of your discussion, consider any IT security implications. **[6]**

- Before processing any **personal data**, Dance17 will need to register with the **Information Commissioner's Office**.

- In order to process personal data there must be a lawful basis. Normally, the lawful basis would be **consent**, however, in this case, the Dance17 will have a contract to provide students with lessons. Their processing can therefore be lawfully carried out as part of delivering this contract.

- Dance17 should only collect the personal **data** that is required for the **purpose** of teaching dance. For example, a name, phone number and email address would be important in order to contact students. Medical information, such as previous injuries would be important in order to keep students safe. Parent information and permissions or consent would also need to be recorded, especially where the children are too young to understand how their personal data is to be used.

- On Dance17's website, they would need to have a **privacy policy** which explains how their students' data will be used. They will also need to ask visitors to the site if they agree to their **cookie policy**.

- Dance17 needs to make sure that their students (**data subjects**) have access to see the data that is stored about them. They also need to **correct any inaccurate data**.

- The data stored is not only personal, but also some of it is very sensitive, such as medical data. It is therefore, very important that **security** precautions are taken such as **encrypting hard drives**, using strong **passwords** and having computers and **backups** locked in a room or safe.

- Dance17 may make use of online services when applying for competitions or sending out emails to students and parents. They need to check that the data does not leave the country unless the protections given are at least as good as those in the UK.

- When a student leaves the academy, their data should be deleted shortly after leaving. Dance17 may need to keep some financial and employment data for legal purposes such as recording how much tax they should pay.

Long answers must be written in paragraphs. Bullet points have been used here to make the answers easier to understand. This type of question will be marked using a Levels Based Marks Scheme. See page 76 for details.

EXAMINATION PRACTICE

BrandSwap is a website that enables its users to sell branded or designer clothes that they no longer want so that others can buy them. They charge a fee for sellers to cover checking the clothes, postage, and costs. Buyers must register with the site before they make a purchase.

Sales at BrandSwap have steadily been increasing and they have now employed Amin to take on the role of Director of Marketing and Social Media.

Before Amin starts, he must sign an acceptable use policy.

(a) Name **two** aspects that the acceptable use policy could cover. [2]

(b) Explain **two** behaviours that may be in the acceptable use policy as acceptable, expected or required by the organisation. [4]

(c) As part of a section on disallowed behaviours, the acceptable use policy states that users may not download or distribute malware.

Describe the sanctions that may be given in the policy if Amin chose to download or distribute malware. [3]

(d) Explain **two** ways in which staff at BrandSwap may be monitored when at work. [4]

The management at BrandSwap have not yet received Amin's signed acceptable use policy. When he starts work, he is unable to access or use any computers.

(e) State **one** reason why Amin cannot use the computers. [1]

One of the first meetings that Amin attends when he starts work is with the Human Resources (HR) Director for BrandSwap. They are concerned about Amin's work/life balance given that he needs to work on social media.

(f) Identify **one** reason that Amin may find it hard to stop working given he is responsible for the company's social media accounts. [1]

Amin has an idea for increasing sales. He will ask visitors to the website to enter their email address. He then intends to use these email addresses to send marketing information about clothes and BrandSwap.

(g) Explain what Amin must do to make sure that this method of marketing is lawful under the Data Protection Act. [2]

In order to collect the email addresses, Amin intends to use a service based in the USA.

(h) Identify **one** potential data protection issue with this. [1]

INFORMATION FLOW DIAGRAMS

Information Flow Diagrams (IFDs) show how information flows between the users or departments of a system or organisation.

Example

IFDs can quickly highlight how organisations operate and the stages involved in various processes within them. This can be useful for staff learning the systems, for example:

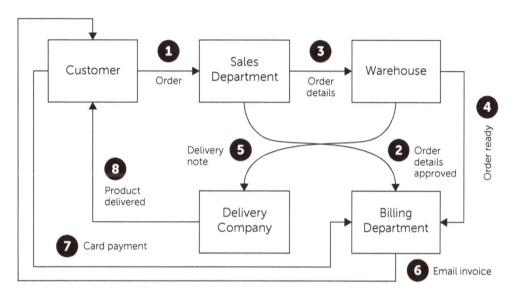

The diagram above shows the order process for an online clothing company.

(a) Identify **two** actions the sales department must take when they receive an order from a customer. [2]

(b) Identify how the delivery company will know there is a new item to be delivered. [1]

(c) Identify what the customer receives before they make a payment for the order. [1]

(a) Sales must pass the order details to the warehouse[1] and the billing department[1] once they have approved the order.

(b) The delivery company are informed of a delivery when the receive a delivery note from the warehouse.[1]

(c) A customer receives an email invoice before they make a payment.[1]

DATA FLOW DIAGRAMS

Organisations use data flow diagrams (DFDs) to illustrate how data moves through their systems. Each person, object or company in a system is known as an entity. The inputs and outputs from both entities and processes are also shown.

Standard symbols

Standard symbols are used in data flow diagrams:

Symbol	Meaning	Example
Entity	An entity is a person, object or company. For example: shop assistant, customer, credit card processor.	Shop assistant
Process	A process is an action that is taken. For example, collect payment, ship product. Processes can be numbered.	1 / Ship product
Data store	A data store may be a file or a database. It is where data is saved and may be numbered.	Order file
Data transferred	Arrows show the direction that data flows. Labels show the data that is transferred.	Login details

A **top level (Level 0)** Data Flow Diagram shows a basic overview of the whole system. It shows how each of the entities interact with the system as one unit. A **Level 1** diagram shows greater detail of internal processes.

Stirrells Garage sells cars through their website. The following occurs when a customer wants to make an offer on a car:

- The customer submits their offer price
- The offer is checked by the sales team
- The offer is accepted or rejected
- The customer is either given a date to collect the car or their offer is rejected

(a) Draw a top level (Level 0) data flow diagram showing the process used for completing a car order. [4]

(b) Once the sales team approve an order, the car needs to be cleaned and polished. When the customer collects the car they must pay by cash. The car sale will be stored in the car database and the payment information will be stored in the finance database.
Draw and label a Level 1 data flow diagram to show these processes. [8]

(a)

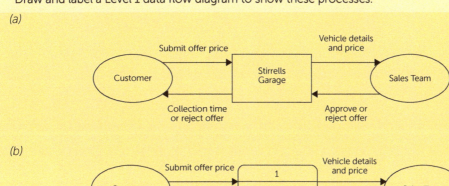

(b)

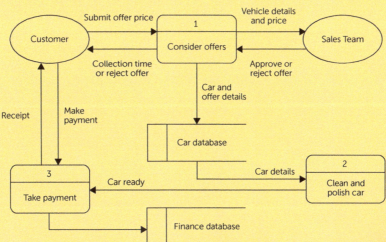

FLOWCHARTS

A flowchart can be used to represent a sequence of steps for a task or process. They are commonly used for troubleshooting problems, to show how a business process works or to design software systems before developers begin writing the program code.

Standard symbols

Standard symbols used in flowcharts are:

Symbol	Meaning
Terminator	A terminator symbol is used to show where the flowchart starts and ends.
Process	A process shows an activity that takes place.
Decision	The outcome of a decision allows different paths to be taken through the flowchart.
Input/Output	Data is input before any processing. The results are then output after processing.
→	Arrows show the direction of flow through the flowchart.

Reams Bookstore offers a 30% discount on children's story books to its members.

Draw a flowchart to show the calculation process. [8]

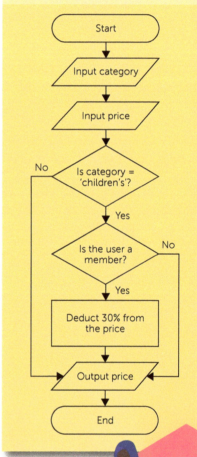

Example

Staff at a company may accidentally delete a cloud-based file.

A flowchart in the company handbook outlines what to do:

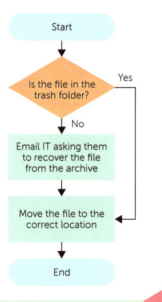

SYSTEM DIAGRAMS

System diagrams show the components of a system and how they work together. A system diagram may show the people that interact with it, the computers, devices and hardware they use and important storage systems such as databases.

Example

This diagram shows how customer support works for a music streaming service. If a customer has a problem they must contact the company through their online chat system. A first line support worker logs the issue. If they cannot resolve it, they pass it to a second line support worker who will fix any problem with the music streaming system. Components and arrows should be labelled.

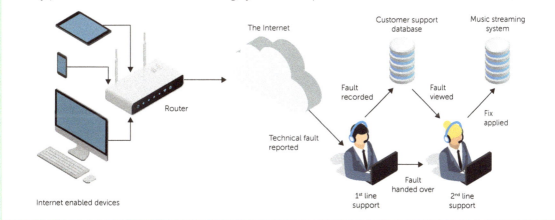

A parking meter issues tickets for parking on a city street for up to an hour. It works as follows:

- The customer inserts coins of at least the value of an hour's parking.
- They then press a button to confirm and issue a ticket.
- The ticket is printed and dispensed to the customer.
- If too much money was inserted, change will be given.
- Before the ticket is confirmed, the customer can press a 'cancel' button to return the coins.

Draw a system diagram to represent the ticket machine. [6]

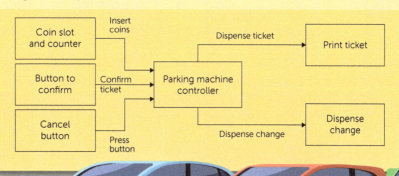

TABLES AND WRITTEN INFORMATION

Organisations commonly use written information in letters, email and reports. It is also used on web pages and marketing communications.

Information can be presented as written text, in a table or graphically. Bar charts or pie charts may represent information well. However, modern infographic styles are even more informative.

Examples

Here are some comparisons:

Annual UK school football injury report

Over the course of a year, each of the football related injuries reported in the UK were logged. The head suffered significantly greater injury than other parts of the body. This is believed to be owing to heading the ball and may include injuries to the head and neck as a result. Ankle and knee injuries were also significant and likely the result of poor tackles and twists of the ankle. Other areas suffered minor injuries.

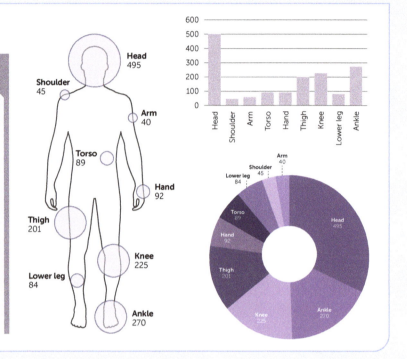

Tables

Tables can be used to present data. The way in which they are presented and sorted can make a difference in the ease of reading and understanding.

A UK annual school football injuries	
Ankle	270
Arm	40
Hand	92
Head	495
Knee	225
Lower leg	84
Shoulder	45
Thigh	201
Torso	89

B UK annual school football injuries	
Head	495
Shoulder	45
Arm	40
Torso	89
Hand	92
Thigh	201
Knee	225
Lower leg	84
Ankle	270

C UK annual school football injuries	
Head	495
Ankle	270
Knee	225
Thigh	201
Hand	92
Torso	89
Lower leg	84
Shoulder	45
Arm	40

State the sort order for each of tables A, B and C. [3]

Table A: Alphabetically by body part[1]. Table B: Descending order of height by body part[1]. Table C: Descending order of injury numbers[1].

INTERPRETING INFORMATION

Information should be presented to tell a story. When interpreting information, ask questions of it and try to draw conclusions. What does it show and why might that be?

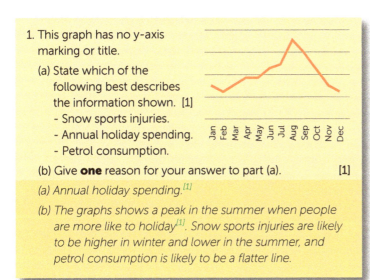

BUS INFORMATION SYSTEM

Station

Route	Destination	Time
508	Briston Road	15:24
12A	City Hall	15:32
139	Cultural Centre	15:41

1. This graph has no y-axis marking or title.
   (a) State which of the following best describes the information shown. [1]
   - Snow sports injuries.
   - Annual holiday spending.
   - Petrol consumption.
   (b) Give **one** reason for your answer to part (a). [1]

   (a) Annual holiday spending.[1]

   (b) The graphs shows a peak in the summer when people are more like to holiday[1]. Snow sports injuries are likely to be higher in winter and lower in the summer, and petrol consumption is likely to be a flatter line.

2. Look at the bus information above.
   (a) State what time the 139 bus to the Cultural Centre is expected to arrive. [1]
   (b) Give **one** reason for using a table to display this information. [1]

   (a) 15:41[1]

   (b) Arrivals are clear[1], easy to sort by time[1] and take up little screen space[1].

PRESENTING KNOWLEDGE AND UNDERSTANDING

This guide describes various ways to present knowledge and information. Choosing the most appropriate way for the situation and purpose is key to telling a story in a way that others can most easily absorb it.

A small cinema is getting a new computer system to automate their ticket sales and reservations. A software developer needs to know exactly how the process works, so that they can create the new system.

Describe how a Data Flow Diagram would be an appropriate way to present this information. [4]

A data flow diagram shows how information flows through the system[1]. It shows each entity[1] and process[1], along with the inputs and outputs[1] from processes. Labelled arrows show where data flows from/to[1]. The developer will understand DFDs so will be able to create the system[1].

CASE STUDY

Sun Solar Installations is a company that fit solar panels to homes. They have a company manual that shows the process of installation as follows:

- A customer contacts the company sales department by email or phone
- A agent arranges a date and time for a site visit – details are sent to the customer by email from the Sales department
- A surveyor carries out site visit
- Parts are ordered from the suppliers
- When the parts arrive the invoice is sent to the accounts department
- Engineers install the parts
- Completion is logged with the accounts department
- The accounts department sends the invoice to the customer

Draw an information flow diagram for the installation process. [8]

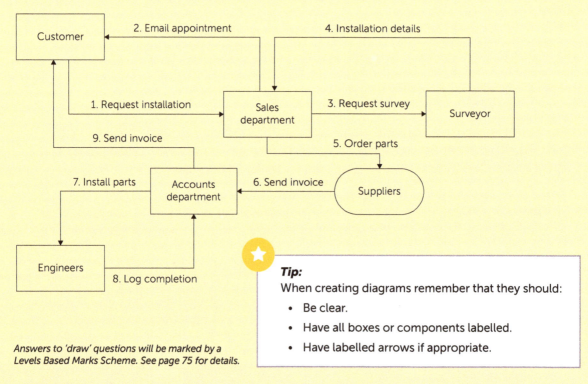

Answers to 'draw' questions will be marked by a Levels Based Marks Scheme. See page 75 for details.

Tip:
When creating diagrams remember that they should:
- Be clear.
- Have all boxes or components labelled.
- Have labelled arrows if appropriate.

EXAMINATION PRACTICE

Sky Land Experience Days (SLED), is an online company that sells vouchers for experience days such as parachuting or white-water rafting. These experiences are then provided by other companies.

The following flowchart has been used by the web development team to determine the final price of a ticket.

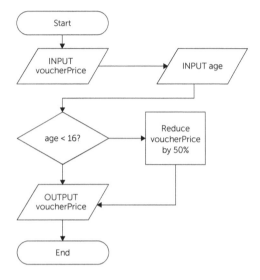

(a) Identify **two** items of data that will be processed in the flowchart. [2]

(b) State the discount that children under 16 get with vouchers. [1]

Some supplier companies find that the cost of giving experiences is the same for children as it is for adults.

(c) Describe how the flowchart could be adapted to make the child discount optional. [2]

The following process occurs when a customer makes an order on the SLED website:

- The customer chooses the experience they want and enters their payment card details
- The payment is processed by the card processor
- The card is accepted or declined
- The customer is given a voucher code or told their card has been declined

The company has created a top level (level 0) data flow diagram to show the above process.

(d) State the entities shown in the data flow diagram. [1]

(e) Annotate the diagram to show the data that is used in the system. [4]

SLED has the following systems diagram to show how their customer support system works.

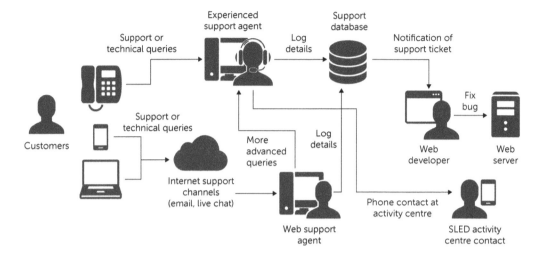

(f) Identify **three** methods that customers can use to contact SLED. [3]

(g) Explain why customers are likely to receive better support if they phone SLED rather than using their computer. [2]

A customer is taking a parachuting experience day. They have arrived at the activity centre, but there is no one there to greet them. They use their smartphone to access SLED through their live chat system.

(h) Describe the process that will occur to resolve the problem. [3]

SLED needs to make sure that it has enough support agents every day to handle customer queries. To cope with staff absence due to sickness, they have the following instructions:

- If an agent is ill and cannot come into work, phone a dedicated support line.
- SLED will then contact 'on call' agents to see if they can come in
- If there are no available agents, then they will contact an agency to hire someone
- If an agent needs time off due to a long-term illness, they should ring the support line.
- Long term absentees are required to give the number of days they expect to be off and an agency will be contacted to hire someone

(i) Draw a flowchart that shows the above process. [8]

EXAMINATION PRACTICE ANSWERS

(a) The data is accessible from any location with an Internet connection (1); It is easy to share files with others (including race competitors who want to see photos or videos) (1); backups will be made by the cloud storage provider(1); files can be synchronised with other employees that are working on them. [2]

(b) She may lose access to her files if her Internet connection is lost (1); she will need to spend time choosing the best cloud provider (1); she may have ongoing storage costs (1); she will need to check that storing the data will be secure / compliant with the Data Protection Act (1). [2]

(c) Cloud storage is scalable / can pay for more storage (1) so the amount of space available can increase as needed (1). [2]

(d) The data will be stored in more than one different physical location / redundancy (1), so if one location has a fire/flood, the data can be recovered from a server in another data centre (1). [2]

(e) The design needs to be responsive/adaptive (1) so that it can display a more appropriate design for different devices / screen orientations (1). Buttons for mobile devices need to be large enough (1) to press with a finger as this is how users will select them (1). Photos that aren't full screen will be hard to see on mobile devices (1) so an option to make them full screen will be needed (1). The website will need to cope with the fact that some features may not be available on the device being used (1) e.g. the use of the user's location data when giving a map (of race venues or her business) (1) – or any other appropriate interface design feature with a corresponding explanation of how it will differ across available devices. [4]

(f) The website/page needs to use HTTPS / Secure Hypertext Transfer Protocol (1). [1]

(g) Kate will be paying for the amount of computer processing that her website uses (1) so if there is an increase in demand, the amount of cloud computing services allocated to her site will increase / the services are scalable (1). This means that there will be more services available to cope with more users/webpage requests (1). Kate will need to pay more for the additional cloud computing services used (1). [3]

(h) They can tether their laptop to their phone (1) using Bluetooth / USB cable (1). This will allow the laptop to access the Internet using their mobile data (1). [2]

(i) The mobile coverage may be poor (1) a transmitter/base station may not be close enough (1). There may be a black spot (1) a hill / building / wall may be blocking the signal (1). The mobile network's infrastructure may be insufficient to cope with the demand of users (1). [2]

(j) The use of WPA/Wi-Fi Protected Access / a Wi-Fi access key (1) will encrypt the connection between the device and Wi-Fi access point (1) which means that if a hacker intercepts the data sent, they won't be able to understand it.(1) [2]

(a) Have a calendar so that the correct date can be clicked (1), have the number of students as a drop down with numbers (1), have a tick-box/checkbox for the number of students (1), explain what happens, or how long they need to wait when the submit button is pressed (1). Use more friendly language for the 'Submit' button – e.g. 'Send enquiry'(1), use a larger font for the title (1), allow users to search for days that are free (1), allow accessible options (1) such as listen to this page (1) or a plus/minus button to increase/decrease the text size (1), provide more information and help to complete the form (1) e.g. which teacher needs to add their name. [4]

(b) Social media (1), live chat (1), voice communication (1). [2]

(c) Customers (1), shareholders (1), students/children (1), parents (1), employees (1). [2]

(d) Video (1) could be used to show other teenagers having fun doing the activities (1), photos/images could show the kayaking that is covered on the course (1), audio (1) could be used to allow students to say what they liked about the day (1). [4]

(e) They won't be able to use mobile phones or computers in the water so will have no interruptions from notifications (1), not have any stress from school/work (1), not need to worry about the infrastructure/mobile signal in the area (1), not need to check or reply to email/private messages (1). [3]

(f) A gantt chart (1) could show the sub-tasks of a project (1) and when they occur (1). An online/cloud calendar (1) could be used to share key events (1). Kan-ban software (1) could be used to show the stages in a project / where schools and customers are in a sales process (1). Planning/project software (1) (such as Teams or Slack) could be used to discuss the progress of projects (1). A shared to-do list (1) would allow everyone to see what tasks need doing and be updated as soon as tasks are complete (1). [4]

(g) Online / cloud office suites / productivity software (1), a blog / website / wiki (which allows multiple users to edit) (1), project software (1) that allows the sharing of information, documents for feedback (1). [1]

(a) Worm, botnet, rootkit, Trojan (horse), spyware (1 mark each). [3]

(b) It is malicious code that infects a host file or program to do harm to a computer or data (1). It replicates itself (1) onto other computers so that they also become infected (1). [2]

(c) The hard drive of a computer is encrypted (1) which means that the data cannot be understood / programs cannot be opened / the computer is unusable (1). A ransom must be paid to the hacker (1) in order to decrypt the hard drive / make the computer usable again (1). [3]

(d) The device could contain a virus / malware (1). When they put it into the USB slot, it may copy the virus / replicate (1) onto the computer system. This will allow the malware to infect more computers on the network / cause damage to the network (1). [2]

(e) There would be damage to the public image of Sekur Systems (especially as they train in this area) (1) which would result in them losing customers (1). If there has been a breach of the Data Protection Act (1) then there may be a fine / financial loss (1). There will be time spent resolving the issue and informing customers (1) which will result in lost productivity for the business (1). The company may be sued / have legal action (1) brought against them if customers have hardship as a result of the data breach (1). [4]

(f) Receptionists are at the front of buildings before anyone goes through a security barrier (1). Any member of the public will therefore be able to shoulder surf (1). As they are in a public area, a visitor could easily be able to walk behind them (1) and notice as they type in a password / have sensitive or personal information on the screen (1). [2]

(g) Text message (1), phone call (1). [1]

(h) An email can be sent that builds trust / urgency / authority (1). This email will request that they send personal information or money (1). There may be the promise of a large amount of money if the person responds (1). The phishing email may have a link to a website (1) where personal/confidential information will be entered and retrieved by the hacker/criminal (1). The email may be attempting to get further information about a particular person in the company so that the criminal/hacker can later target them (1) – this is known as spear phishing (1). [3]

(i) [3]

(a) A barrier to access beyond the reception area (1), a physical lock to enter the building (opened with a swipe card, RFID card or key), a security guard (1), locked server/network rooms (1). [2]

(b) 'Something you know': password / PIN / personal ID number / passphrase / answer to a question – such as your first school's name / your date of birth (1). 'Something you have': a bank card / an RFID tag / a mobile phone (for sending text messages with an authentication code) / a passport / a drivers licence (1). [2]

(c) When the user asks to send the money, the app can ask for their fingerprint to be scanned (something they are) (1), a password to be entered (something they know) (1), they could send a text message to their phone with an authentication code (something they have) (1), they could ask for letters from a password (something they know), they could ask the user to use a card reader for an authentication code (something they have) (1) – Any two answers that are from two different factors. [2]

(d)   [4]

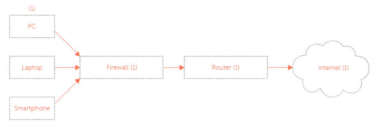

1 mark for all of the left three boxes – any combination of PC/laptop/smartphone/tablet/desktop.
1 mark for each of the other three boxes. Router must be next to Internet.
1 mark for correctly drawn arrows.

(e) A white-hat hacker (1) will be employed to try to find vulnerabilities in the network / computers (1). They may for instance, check that they cannot successfully carry out a brute-force attack on passwords (1) or they may try default passwords (1). They may test that unused ports on servers are blocked (1). They will also check that software is up to date and has the most recent security updates applied (1).   [3]

(f) The protocol used will be HTTPS / Hypertext Transfer Protocol Secure (1), a padlock symbol appears by the web address (1), the address bar will turn green (1), they can check the security certificate for the website (to see it is valid) (1).   [2]

Section B3

(a) Even though the staff are temporary, they will still need strong passwords (1) as they are using payment systems / ride control systems (1). At the end of the six months, temporary staff will need their accounts to be locked / passwords changed (1) so that they cannot be used after they leave (1).
The password policy / acceptable use policy will need to explain that staff cannot share passwords (1) to help minimise the risks of staff/public misusing computers (1).   [4]

(b) If a member of staff is at a till and they leave for more than 10 seconds then a member of the public would have enough time (1) to open the till / apply a discount (1).
If a ride control system is unlocked for longer than 10 seconds with no one near it, then it could be tampered with / a ride launched (1) which could put the ride out of action / compromise the safety of rides (1).   [2]

(c) Apply security patches (1), install antivirus software (1), install software firewalls (1), configure security settings (1), configure user access to files/programs (1), prevent users from installing programs (1), prevent users from accessing the Internet if they don't need it for the job (1), encrypt drives / backups (1).   [2]

(d) Flood (1), fire (1), earthquake (1), hurricane (1), cyber attack (1).   [2]

(e) Temporary files / cached files / files in a recycle bin (1) as these would be lost with time anyway / as these won't be needed to restore the system and data (1). The operating system / program software (1) as these can be reinstalled from the original installation media / downloads (1). Unimportant photos/videos that they don't mind losing (1) as media files tend to take up lots of storage space (1).   [2]

(f) Removable magnetic hard disk (1) / solid state drive (1), tape drive (1), Blu-ray disk (1), DVD (1), USB flash media (1).   [3]

(g) Data protection officer (1).   [1]

(h) Safety systems will have been the most important to deal with first (1) for example, any computer systems that are responsible for fire alarms and detectors / the management of gates to rides or the theme park (1). Next in the timeline would be systems that control rides (1) as without these, the theme park still cannot open (1). Then, computer systems that are used for ticket entry (1) so that the park can open (1). Next, the payment systems for restaurants will need to be restored (1) so that the restaurants can open (1). Some important systems for the management of the park may be a high priority (1), such as their email system and phone system (1). The systems used by their marketing department will probably be the last to be restored(1) as there is no need to market a theme park until it is able to open (1).   [3]

(a) Customer name (1), appointment time (1), appointment date (1), duration of the appointment (1), services that the customer needs (1), email address (1), telephone number (1). [4]

(b) The Data Protection Act says that personal information must be processed / used in a reasonable way (1). Having data such as name and phone number (1) displayed publicly reduces the expected level of privacy a customer would expect (1) and could be a breach of the Data Protection Act resulting in a fine / loss of reputation (1). [2]

(c) Access can be restricted (1) by using a fingerprint / password (1). The data stored on the tablet will be constantly updated (1), meaning that hairdressers won't be waiting for customers that have cancelled (1). Staff may be able to use the tablet to contact customers (1) if there is a problem with an appointment or they need to cancel it (1). A hard copy / print out uses paper which needs trees/forests to be destroyed (1), whereas a digital copy has less environmental impact (1). [4]

(d) The customers belong to Abigail's salon (1). Luna only had access to this list by working for the salon (1) and this data is an asset / property of the Salon (1). Taking the customer list to encourage customers to leave would therefore not be ethical (1). [2]

(e) Legally, this would be data theft (1) or a breach of the Data Protection Act (1) as it was sent outside the salon business / as it was sent to an email address that doesn't have a reasonable level of security for the personal data (1). Luna is likely to have a contract that says she cannot do this (1) so she would now be in breach of contract (1). [2]

(f) The manufacture of the new tablet (1) will require energy / rare materials (1). The disposal of the system may lead to toxic materials going into landfill / may require energy and chemicals to recycle correctly (1). Buying a new tablet / disposing of the old tablet will have transport costs (1) which use energy and contribute to carbon emissions (1). [4]

(g) She could make the computer auto power off (1) at the end of each day (1). She could set the computer to automatically suspend (1) when it hasn't been used for a while so that the hard disk stops rotating / CPU stops processing (1) until a key / the power button is pressed (1). She could reduce the brightness of the screen (1). [3]

(a) Desktop computers (1), tablets (1), phones (1), mobiles (1), printers (1), the computer network (1), documents (1), knowledge (1). [2]

(b) Lock computer when you are away from it (1) so that the account can't be used by others (1). Use a strong password (1) so that it is difficult for others to guess / a brute-force attack (1). Use polite/professional language/tone (1) in all communications/email/social media posts (1). Inform the network administrator of any suspicious email (1) as it may contain a virus / malware / be a phishing attempt (1). [4]

(c) He may have a disciplinary hearing / investigation (1) that results in a verbal or written warning (1) or the termination of his employment (1). Given the severity of this behaviour, it may also be reported to the police (1). As the intentional spreading of malware is against the law / The Police and Justice Act (2016) (1), he could end up with a criminal conviction (1). [3]

(d) CCTV can record their actions in and around the building (1) to reduce the chance of theft / prove where they are at a given time (1). Logs of when users log in/out will be stored (1) which can show which user/account was used in any breach of the computer system or network (1). The time of entry/exit to the building can be logged (1) to verify when employees start or end work / to find potential people that may have carried out / seen an unacceptable behaviour (1). Logs of web usage may be monitored (1) to see if inappropriate sites are being visited(1). Emails may be archived / accessed (1) to monitor usage / investigate misuse (1). Logs of use of social media/websites can be monitored to see if they are having a negative impact on professional work (1). [4]

(e) BrandSwap's company policy requires that no employees shall be given computer access until the AUP is signed and received (1). Passwords are only allocated on receipt of a signed agreement (1). [1]

(f) Social media allows people to respond/criticise the company any time of day or night (1) and typically users expect very fast feedback (1) so Amin would be under pressure to work long hours and solve problems very quickly, even if he were at home (1). [1]

(g) He will need to get the consent (1) of visitors before he can store their email addresses / send out any emails (1). He must explain (in a privacy policy) how people's data will be used (1). [2]

(h) Data cannot be transferred / stored in a country with less protection than the UK. (1) (Amin will need to be careful to check that the protections of the data are sufficient). [1]

(a) voucherPrice (1), age (1). [2]

(b) Half price / 50% off (1). [1]

(c) A second decision symbol could be placed before the age < 16 symbol (1). This would ask if the supplier wants to apply the discount (1). If they do then the discount would be applied (1). [2]

(d) Customer and card processor (1). [1]

(e) [4]

(f) Phone (1), email (1), live chat (1). [3]

(g) They will get through to an 'experienced support agent' (1) who deals with 'more advanced queries' (1) from a 'web support agent' (1). [2]

(h) A web support agent will respond to the live chat (1). As the SLED activity centre will need to be contacted, they will forward the issue to a more experienced support agent (1) who will log the details in the support database (1). The agent will then contact the activity centre by phone (1) to resolve the issue. [3]

(i) [8]

Draw questions are marked by a levels-based mark scheme as follows:

Level	Mark	Descriptor
0	0	No answer given or nothing relevant has been drawn
1	1–2	• Limited use of appropriate symbols • Limited use of appropriate arrows and direction of data / information flow • Limited coverage of the scenario requirements
2	3–5	• Some use of appropriate symbols • Some use of appropriate arrows and direction of data / information flow • Some coverage of the scenario requirements
3	6–8	• Mostly accurate use of appropriate symbols • Mostly accurate use of appropriate arrows and direction of data / information flow • Mostly accurate coverage of the scenario requirements

The above descriptors have been written in simple language to give an indication of the expectations of each mark band. See the Pearson BTEC website for the official mark schemes used.

LEVELS BASED MARK SCHEME FOR EXTENDED RESPONSE QUESTIONS

Questions that require extended writing use mark bands. The whole answer will be marked together to determine which mark band it fits into and which mark should be awarded within the mark band. The first two bullet points are the same for all extended response questions. The final bullet depends on the type of question asked.

Level	6-mark discuss questions	9-mark assess question	12-mark evaluate question	Descriptor
	0	0	0	No answer given or none of the points are relevant to the question
1	1–2 marks	1–3 marks	1–4 marks	• Some isolated knowledge and understanding has been shown, but there are major gaps in the response • Few of the points made are relevant to the context of the question • **Discuss questions:** there is little discussion. Different aspects and viewpoints haven't been considered • **Assess questions:** there is a limited assessment with generic points. Relevant factors or events and their relative importance are not considered. This leads to a weak conclusion • **Evaluation questions:** A limited evaluation is given which leads to an unsupported or weak conclusion.
2	3–4 marks	4–6 marks	5–8 marks	• Some accurate knowledge and understanding has been shown. Only minor gaps in the response • Some of the points made are relevant to the context of the question, but the link isn't always clear • **Discuss questions:** Different aspects have been considered. How the aspects relate or connect to each other is sometimes shown • **Assess questions:** there is an assessment which considers the relevant factors or events and their relative importance. These support the final conclusion • **Evaluation questions:** A partially developed evaluation that shows different points of view even if not always in detail. This partially supports the conclusion.
3	5–6 marks	7–9 marks	9–12 marks	• Mostly accurate and detailed knowledge and understanding • Most points made are relevant to the context in the question. Clear links are made between points • **Discuss questions:** A well-developed and logical discussion is given. A range of different aspect have been considered. How the aspects relate or connect to each other is considered throughout • **Assess questions:** there is a well-developed assessment which clearly considers relevant factors or events and their relative importance. These support the conclusion given • **Evaluation questions:** A well-developed evaluation that is logical and covers different points of view in detail. This fully supports the conclusion.

The above descriptors have been written in simple language to give an indication of the expectations of each mark band. See the Pearson BTEC website for the official mark schemes used.

INDEX

Symbols

4G data 5
5G 4
24/7/365 17

A

Acceptable Use Policy 41, 54
accessibility 21, 23
access levels 35
access rights 6
ad hoc network 2
age filtering 8
alt text 21
anti-virus software 36, 44
attack
  cyber 28
  five-stage action plan 43
attribution 57
authentication 35
autocomplete 36
autosaving 8

B

backup 6, 14, 36, 39, 42, 44, 59
bandwidth 5
base station 4
behaviour analysis 38
biometrics 35
black-hat hacker 30, 38
blackspots 4
Bluetooth 2
blurring of boundaries 55
Botnet 30
broadband 4, 12
buttons 21

C

CAPTCHA 36
cellular network 4
chat 7
  chat bots 19
  chat rooms 20

cloud 5, 39
  applications 8
  computing 7
  platforms 8
  services 9, 12, 14
  storage 6
  technology 11
co-authoring 7
collaboration tools 7, 18, 23
collaborative working 14
colour blindness 21
colour schemes 21
command verbs vi
communication
  channels 19
  platforms 19, 20
  tools 18
compatibility, cloud software 12
computer platform 8
Computer Misuse Act (1990) 58
consistency, software versions 7
cookie 47
Copyright, Designs and Patents
      Act 1988 57
criminal use 58
cultures 16
cyber-attack 43
cybersecurity 28, 50

D

damage to public image 32
data
  centre 6, 11
  exchange 47
  flow diagrams 62
  level protection 36
  Protection Act 39, 47, 50, 56
  recovery 44
  security 11, 29
  subject rights 56
Denial of service (DoS) 30
depression 26
developed countries 4
developing countries 4
device hardening 36, 41
device synchronisation 10
digital divide 52

digital footprint 46
direct messages 19, 20
disaster recovery 11, 42
  five-stage plan 43
disclosure of data 29
dispersed data 23
distributed data 23, 39
diversity 16
dongle 4
downloads from the Internet 29
downtime 6, 12, 32, 42
dual-coding iii

E

Ebbinghaus iii
electronic
  distribution 49
  waste 48
email 19
employees 16
encryption 37, 39, 59
  WPA 3
environment, responsibilities 48
equal access 52
Equality Act 2010 52
espionage 28, 33
ethical hacking 38
external threats 30

F

face recognition 35
fibre optics 4, 5
fingerprint recognition 35
firewall 36, 50
flexible working 17, 22, 25
flowcharts 64
fonts 21
forms of notation 66

G

Gantt chart 20
Global Positioning Systems 46
graphs 67
grey hat hackers 38

H

hacking 30, 38
health 22
  and safety 48
home working 25, 26
hotspot 2
HTTPS 37

I

inclusivity 17, 21, 22
incremental backup 42
individuals 25
Information Commissioner 50
information flow diagrams 61
infrastructure 4, 24, 52
instant messaging 7
intellectual property 57
interface design 9, 21
internal threats 29
Internet Service Provider (ISP) 53
interpreting information 67
Intranet 19

K

keylogger 33
keypads 35

L

layout and design 9
legislation 58
licencing 57
live chat 19
location based data 46
logs 44
loneliness 26

M

maintenance 12
malware 31, 44, 58
man-in-the-middle attack 30
manufacture of IT systems 48
mining 48
mirror 42
mobile coverage 4
modern teams 16, 18
monitoring 54
multicultural teams 16, 22

N

navigation buttons 21
net neutrality 53
network 2
  ad hoc 2
  availability 4
  downtime 6
  open Wi-Fi 2
  security 3
notifications 10

O

obscuring data 36
offline working 10
online applications 7
online working 10
open networks 3, 4
operating system 8
outsourcing 14

P

paid for vs free services 9
password policy 41
passwords 35, 59
patents 57
penetration testing 38
performance considerations 12
performance issues, networks 3
permissions 44, 57
personal
  area network (PAN) 2
  data 56, 59
  hotspot 2
pharming 30
phishing 30
physical security 35
planning tools 18
policies 41, 49
portable storage devices 29
power saving 49
privacy 47
private message 19
productivity 26, 32
professional standards 52
public status updates 19

R

ransomeware 31
rare materials 48
recovery procedures 36
recycling 49
redundancy 11
registered trademarks 57
remote working 22, 25, 26
replacing systems 48
reporting concerns 41
responsibilities 41
responsible use of data 47
responsive design 21
retinal scanning 35
retrieval practice iii
RFID (radio frequency ID) 35
right to be forgotten 56
rootkit 31

S

sanctions, acceptable use 54
scalability 6, 8
scheduling tools 18
screen
  brightness 49
  readers 21
  sharing 7
security 11, 59
  breach, impact of 32
  controls 29
  external threats 30
  internal threats 29
  parameters 41
  physical 35
  policies 41
serif fonts 21
server outage 12
settings policies 49
sharing data 46, 47
shoulder surfing 30
sleep mode 49
social engineering 30
social media 19, 55
Software as a Service (SaaS) 8
software interface design 36
software updates 14
spyware 31, 33
staff 16
stakeholder 19
standards 52

streaming 53
symbols
  data flow diagrams 62
  flowcharts 64
synchronisation 6, 10, 14
system
  attacks 28
  data analysis 38
  diagrams 65
  security 38

T

tables 66
technologies
  modern 16
  modern, impacts of 22, 24, 25
tethering 2
text-to-speech 21
The Police and Justice Act 58
time zones 16, 20
trademarks 57
transactional data 46
transmitter 4
Trojans 31
two-factor authentication 35

U

unauthorised access 58
untrustworthy websites 29
upgrading systems 48
UPS (Uninterruptible Power
    Supply) 6
uptime 12
usage and settings 49
user access restriction 35

V

verification 35
version
  history 18
  recovery 11
video conferencing 7, 19
Virtual Private Network (VPN) 5
virtual storage 8
virus 29, 31
voice communication 19
VoIP (Voice over Internet
    Protocol) 19

W

Waste Electrical and Equipment
    Regulations (WEEE) 48
websites 19
wellbeing 26
white hat hackers 38
white space 21
working styles 25
worms 31
written information 66

EXAMINATION TIPS

With your examination practice, use a boundary approximation using the following table. Be aware that boundaries are usually a few percentage points either side of this.

Grade	L1 Pass	L1 Merit	L1 Distinction	L2 Pass	L2 Merit	L2 Distinction
Boundary	25%	30%	40%	50%	65%	80%

1. Read each question carefully. You will get no marks for giving an answer to a question you think is appearing rather than the actual question. Avoid simply rewriting a question in your answer or repeating examples that are already given in the question.

2. Full answers should be given to questions – not just key words or bullet points.

3. Read the context of the question carefully. Make sure your answer then matches this context.

4. Give, state and name questions require you to recall a short piece of key information. No explanation is required. There will be one mark for each point you make.

5. Where two examples are asked for, avoid giving two similar examples. For example, if you are asked to give two methods to keep data secure, avoid giving both keypads and locks as these are both examples of physical security methods. Locks and encryption would be a better answer as they are different examples.

6. Remember that explain questions have two marks for each point. You need to make a point or example for the first mark, and then expand it with a linked explanation for the second mark. To help you justify your responses, aim to include words such as 'because' or 'so'.

7. Describe questions require an answer that gives a number of steps or points. If three marks are given for the question, then three steps or points will be needed in the answer.

8. Long answer questions use the command verbs discuss, assess or evaluate. Plan these answers first. This will keep your answer focused and avoid repeating information. It will also help you to make clear links between your points and come to a conclusion where needed.

9. Be careful with vague answers. For cloud storage benefits it is not acceptable to write that it 'has more space' or 'costs less'. Better answers would be 'it allows access to a larger amount of storage capacity' or 'it allows the purchase of a cheaper computer with less storage capacity'.

10. If the question and context mention how an issue affects an organisation, make sure that the answer refers to organisations and not individuals.

11. Circle or underline key parts of the question that will help you when answering it. For instance, you may circle that the context is talking about an organisation or individual, or the number of examples that you need to give.

12. Learn the correct symbols required for flowcharts and data flow diagrams. Label all diagrams, showing the flows of data or direction of flow with labelled arrows. If a question asks you to "annotate the diagram to explain how...", then make sure that you both annotate the diagram and explain the features asked for in the question.

Good luck!

www.ingramcontent.com/pod-product-compliance
Lightning Source LLC
LaVergne TN
LVHW060400080326
832902LV00046B/4624